An Inspirational Treasury of
D. L . MOODY

COMPILED & WRITTEN BY
STANLEY BARNES

AMBASSADOR

Belfast Northern Ireland **Greenville** South Carolina

An Inspirational Treasury of D. L. Moody
© Copyright 2000 Stanley Barnes

ISBN 1 84030 083 3

Ambassador Publications
a division of
Ambassador Productions Ltd.
Providence House
Ardenlee Street,
Belfast,
BT6 8QJ
Northern Ireland
www.ambassador-productions.com

Emerald House
427 Wade Hampton Blvd.
Greenville
SC 29609, USA
www.emeraldhouse.com

CONTENTS

INTRODUCTION *5*

1   D. L. MOODY – THE MAN AND HIS MESSAGE *7*

2   SELECTED SAYINGS OF D. L. MOODY *15*

3   LIVING INSIGHTS AND ILLUSTRATIONS *41*

4   THE FINEST OF THE WHEAT –
     EXCERPTS FROM MOODY'S SERMONS *67*

5   THE BEST OF MOODY'S SERMONS *93*
     The New Birth – John 3 v 3
     Weighed in the Balance – Daniel 5 v 27
     Excuses – Luke 14 v 18
     Heaven and Who are There – Luke 10 v 20

6   WHY GOD USED D. L. MOODY –
     A SERMON BY DR. R. A. TORREY *133*

INTRODUCTION

D. L. MOODY'S FAVOURITE TEXT WAS "...BUT HE THAT DOETH THE WILL OF GOD ABIDETH FOR EVER." I JOHN 2:17. Regrettably the world forgets all to quickly the memories of the lives and labours of those who have lived to do the will of God. Indeed many of today's generation will know little or nothing of the evangelist Dwight Lyman Moody.

This Inspirational Treasury is not a life story of Moody, but rather an attempt to gather together some of the lessons that he himself learned during his lifetime that will perhaps be an inspiration to others so that they too will yield themselves to a life of surrender and service.

The words of the evangelist Henry Varley, "The world has yet to see what God can do with and for and through and in a man who is fully and wholly consecrated to Him," are still true and relevant for the man and woman of today.

Moody's success as an evangelist was founded upon his love for the Word of God, his infilling of the Holy Spirit and his vision for the lost.

This Treasury pulsates with that divinely inspired vision.

Stanley Barnes
Hillsborough, Co. Down
June 2000

1

D. L. MOODY
THE MAN AND HIS MESSAGE

'MOODY IS DEAD.' THIS SCREAMING BANNER HEADLINE OF THE NEW YORK *WORLD* EVENING EDITION of December 22, 1899, was only one of thousands of news bulletins sent around the world, announcing the death of one of the greatest evangelists who ever lived. The editor of the Chicago *Times Herald* wrote in his editorial on December 23, *'The greatest evangelist of the century has passed away.'* Many other newspapers also printed wonderful eulogies about this great man who had made such an impact on the lives of so many thousands of people, but while many mourned his passing, let us not forget what Moody himself said concerning his death, "Some day you will read in the papers that D. L. Moody of East Northfield, is dead. Don't you believe a word of it! At that moment I shall be more alive than I am now. I shall have gone up higher that is all; out of this old clay tenement into a house that is immortal – a body that death cannot touch, that sin cannot taint, a body fashioned like unto His glorious body. I was born of the flesh in 1837. I was born of the spirit in 1855. That which is born of the flesh may die. That which is born of the spirit will live forever."

Dwight Lyman Moody was born at Northfield, Massachusetts on February 5 1837. The young Victoria was crowned Queen of England when he was four months old, and later in life many of Moody's Campaigns in Great Britain caught her attention and she wrote of Moody and his songwriter Sankey, "I am sure that they are good and sincere people, but it is not the sort of religious performance which I like."

Life for the Moody household was far from easy. His father was a heavy drinker and he died suddenly when Dwight was only four years old, and so for the fatherless family of six boys and two girls there were many hardships. Years later they looked back with gratitude to the assistance given by relations and also the minister of Northfield Unitarian Church, the Rev. Oliver Everett. He not only gave them material help, but also encouraged Betty Moody 'not to part with the children but keep them together as best she could, to trust in God, and to bring them up for Him.'

In 1854, just a few weeks after his seventeenth birthday, he told his mother: "I am tired of this, and I am not going to stay around here any longer. I am going to the city." He headed for Boston, and went to work in his uncle's shoe shop. His Uncle Sam tried to encourage him and made him promise that he would attend Sunday school and church services on a regular basis and it was Moody's Sunday school teacher, Edward Kimball who was to win him for Christ on Saturday 21 April 1855. On that day, Kimball felt a great burden upon him that he should go and visit Moody at the shoe shop. In a back room of the store he told Moody of Christ's love for him and the love Christ wanted in return, and he had the great joy of pointing him to a personal faith in the Saviour. "I was in a new world," said Moody. "I thought the old sun shone a good deal brighter than it ever had before. I thought it was just smiling upon me; and as I walked out upon Boston Common, and heard the birds singing in the trees, I thought they were all singing a song to me. Do you know I fell in love with the birds. I had never cared for them before. It seemed to me I was in love with all creation. I had not a bitter feeling against any man, and I was ready to take all men to my heart." Such was the joy he experienced, as he trusted Christ for salvation.

A month later he applied for membership in the Mount Vernon Congregational Church. His application was refused on the grounds that there was no solid evidence of his new birth, and that his knowledge of the Scriptures was abysmal. He was again examined on March 12, 1856 and on May 3 he was received into membership of the church.

Four months later, without telling any of his family, he moved to Chicago, more than a thousand miles from his home town and after he arrived, he sent off a quick note telling them that "God is the same here as in Boston." He managed to get a job as a shoe salesman with the Wiswall Company on Lake Street. He joined the Plymouth Congregational Church, rented five pews and filled them Sunday after Sunday. He also got involved in the Sunday school work, and began by walking into a little mission on North Wells Street and informing the superintendent that he wanted to teach a class. The superintendent told him that he had almost as many teachers as students, and Moody impulsively decided to recruit his own class, and to the amazement of the superintendent and other teachers he showed up with eighteen pupils.

"That was the happiest Sunday school I have ever known" Moody later recalled, "I had found out what my mission was."

As the work grew, he rented a beer hall on North Market Street in an area known as 'Little Hell,' and Moody filled it with more than 500 each Sunday.

He became known as Crazy Moody because of his amazing ability as a soul winner. The members of the Sunday school very quickly increased to fifteen hundred boys and girls.

The word of Moody's success soon reached Abraham Lincoln, the president-elect, and on his way from Springfield to Washington, D.C. for his first inauguration, he called in to see Moody. As he was leaving, he told the Sunday school children, 'put into practice what you learn from your teachers, some of you may one day become president of the United States.'

Unknown to Moody and those around him, his experience as a Sunday school worker was but part of God's preparation for his life's work in winning the lost to Jesus Christ. The sermons which he preached to the children, and his natural ability to speak simply and sincerely from the heart, allowed Moody to succeed where others had failed. Years later Moody, reflecting on his own practical training, said: "If every minister of the Gospel had the same training as I went through, there would not be such long sermons preached or so many empty seats. I preached for years in the army and on the streets, and I learned to say what I had to say rapidly and forcibly, backing up my points with apt illustrations, just as Christ enforced his sayings with striking parables. This is the way to keep an audience interested."

Moody was the means of starting the movement of the Young Men's Christian Association. He became a missionary for the Chicago YMCA and was for a time the president. Soon the YMCA and his Sunday school took up much of his time, and as he reached and won more and more converts, he realised that he needed to have a church where they could be nourished. In 1864, he opened the Illinois Street Independent Church, which seated 1,500. J. H. Harwood was called to be their pastor and Moody served as one of its deacons.

In 1867, Moody took his first trip to Great Britain. It was meant to be a vacation, during which time he visited the Metropolitan Tabernacle and sat under the ministry of C. H. Spurgeon. He also met the renowned George Muller, but the man who made the biggest impression on him was Harry Moorhouse, the 'boy preacher' from Lancashire, who taught him to preach the love of God.

In 1871, Moody's church, his home and the YMCA were all destroyed in the tragedy of the great fire of Chicago. In the following weeks he built a new church, the Northside Tabernacle, which was turned into a relief centre, feeding and clothing thousands of people who had lost everything when their homes were destroyed.

Soon Moody felt that God was once again calling him to take his ministry further afield. He teamed up with Ira Sankey, a former internal revenue agent, and now a full time song leader for Moody, and in1873 they accepted an invitation to visit Great Britain to take the message of the Gospel to the people there. At first the audiences found it difficult to get used to his accent, even his bad grammar and his different style of preaching, but the Holy Spirit began to work in the hearts and minds of the people and his campaigns went on for many months. They then travelled up to Scotland where it was said that one day he preached to an estimated 50,000 people outdoors from a buggy. Ireland was next on their itinerary, and after preaching to huge audiences in Belfast they returned to London, where the crowds exceeded 2.5 million, such was the spirit of revival.

On returning to America they held campaigns that took them to Chicago, Boston, Cleveland, Cincinnati, Richmond, Denver, St. Louis and San Francisco.

His ability to win souls for Christ, which began, with his first efforts at soul winning in Chicago among children, was evident both in America and Britain. It was said of him by an Anglican minister, that 'he put one hand on Britain and the other on America and lifted them both nearer to God.'

W. H. Daniels, who compiled a book of Moody's sermons, referred to the fact that Moody customarily spoke on the 'three R's' of the Bible, and that his evangelistic campaigns where structured around these.

Ruined by the Fall

The gospel message for Moody began with the fact that Adam's sin made everyone absolutely helpless and morally corrupt. "There are no naturally good men..." Moody said. "The natural man I declare to be morally unsound from the crown of his head to the sole of his foot." Human efforts to heal spiritual helplessness and sinfulness are doomed to failure. "We may try to patch up our old Adam nature, but it is of no use. It will be a failure. Men have tried to do it for six thousand years, and what God cannot do, men need not try. God has said that it is bad.... When I was born of my parents in 1837, I received my human nature from them, and it was a very bad nature, too. The nature they received from their forefathers was bad also, and we might trace it right back to Adam. You might say that the earth is a vast hospital. Every man and woman coming into it needs a physician. If you search, you will find everyone wounded. By nature we are sinners."

Redeemed by the Blood

Christ and His Cross were central in his message. He said, "There is nothing, my friends, that brings out the love of God like the cross of Christ, it tells of the breadth, the length, and the height of his love. If you want to know how much God loves you, you must go to Calvary to find out."

In his famous sermon 'The Blood' he said, "I can't find anything to tell me the way to heaven but by the blood. This book (holding up the bible) wouldn't be worth carrying home if you take the silver thread out of it. The blood commences in Genesis and goes on to Revelation. That is what this book is written for. It tells its own story; and if a man should come and preach another gospel, don't you believe him. If an angel should come and preach anything else, don't believe it. Don't trifle with the subject of the Blood. In your dying hour you would give more to be sheltered behind this Blood than for all the world."

"If you will read your Bible in the light of Calvary, you will find there is no other way of coming to heaven but by the blood. The devil does not fear 'ten thousand' preachers who preach a bloodless religion. A man who preaches a bloodless religion is doing the devil's work and I don't care who he is."

Regenerated by the Spirit

Throughout his evangelistic efforts Moody placed great emphasis upon the Person and work of the Holy Spirit in regeneration. He said, "The Holy Spirit is the world's greatest evangelist."

He believed the Holy Spirit was responsible for the conviction and conversion of the soul. "Every dead soul is brought to life by the power of the Spirit...."

There was never the slightest doubt as to what Moody believed and preached. These three great truths impressed upon him the necessity and possibility of salvation and his responsibility to win the lost for Christ.

"I look upon this world as a wrecked vessel," he said, "God has given me a lifeboat, and said to me, 'Moody save all you can.'"

Robert L. Duffus, one of Moody's greatest admirers was quoted as saying, "Moody in his race to save souls travelled more than a million miles, addressed more than a hundred million people, and personally prayed and pleaded with 750,000 sinners. All in all, it is very probable that he reduced the population of hell by a million souls."

Moody, the Man and his Message has left the Church of Christ, as it faces the challenge of reaching the unreached in the new millennium, a timeless legacy, for God can still do today what He did through Moody.

Henry Varley's words are still valid today; 'the world has yet to see what God can do with and for and through and in a man who is fully and wholly consecrated to Him.'

2

SELECTED SAYINGS OF
D. L. MOODY

D. L. MOODY ONCE SAID "THERE'S ONE PROFESSIONAL
CHAIR I WANT TO SEE ENDOWED IN ENGLAND AND IN
the United States, and that is a chair of common sense. If you ever
hear of my leaving money to endow a chair in a college it will be
one to teach common sense."

Judging from his writings and preaching, he would have been
the right person to occupy such a chair. For example he once said,
"I would rather have ten men do the work of one man than one man
do the work of ten."

Below is a collection of Moody's short sayings that have been
gathered from a wide range of sources and arranged under various
topics for the convenience of pastors, teachers and speakers. They

will provide a rich resource of valuable material that is still fresh and relevant to today's generation.

Afflictions

- Afflictions are but the shadows of God's wings. The darker the night, the brighter the stars. The hotter the fire, the purer the gold.

- We can stand affliction better than we can prosperity, for in prosperity we forget God.

Ambition

- No worldly gain can satisfy the human heart. Roll the whole world in and still there would be room.

Answer

- God will answer your cry in His own good time.

Assurance

- Do you believe the Lord will call a poor sinner, and then cast him out? His word stands forever; "Him that cometh unto me I will in no wise cast out."

Attitude

- Be careful for nothing, prayerful for everything, thankful for anything.

Backslider

- There is one thing about a backslider, he is always finding fault with church members.

- I will challenge you to find a father or mother that has backslidden whose children haven't gone to ruin.

- I think the hardest people to reach are the sons and daughters of backsliders.

- If you treated God as a personal friend there would not be a backslider.

Bait

- Use bait that the fish like.

Behaviour

- A Christian is the world's Bible – and some of them need revising.

Bible

- What we need today is men who believe in the Bible from the crown of their heads to the soles of their feet, who believe in the whole of it, the things they understand in it and the things they do not understand.

- There's no better book with which to defend the Bible than the Bible itself.

- I know the Bible is inspired because it inspires me.

- The study of God's Word brings peace to the heart. In it, we find a light for every darkness, life in death, the promise of our Lord's return, and the assurance of everlasting glory.

- I never saw a useful Christian who was not a student of the Bible. If a person neglects the Bible there is not much for the Holy Spirit to work with. We must have the Word.

- God did not give us the Scriptures to increase our knowledge, but to change our lives.

- The Bible is the only news book in the world. The newspaper tells what has taken place, but this book tells us what will take place.

- It is easier for me to have faith in the Bible than to have faith in D. L. Moody, for Moody has fooled me lots of times.

- It is God's Word, not our comment on it that saves souls.

Blessing

- The daybreak blessing is a daylong gain. Seek the heavenly manna in the morning of your life.

- I am sick of hearing people asking for crumbs from God's table. Crumbs are good enough for cats and dogs, not for sons and daughters.

Blood

- No matter how fast the colour is the Blood of Jesus Christ can wash it out.

Call

- If God calls us to a work He can qualify us to do it.

- One reason why so many break down in the pulpit is because they run before they are sent, in fact before they are called at all, and the result is so many failures.

Character

- If I take care of my character, my reputation will take care of itself.

- Character is what a man is in the dark.

Chastening

- By chastening, the Lord separates the sin that He hates from the sinner whom He loves.

Children

- Children old enough to sin are old enough to repent. Satan does not wait till the children grow up – why should you?

Church Attendance

- Church attendance is as vital to a disciple as a transfusion of rich, healthy blood to a sick man.

Clean Vessels

- The Master will only employ clean vessels to convey the water of life to thirsty souls.

Commands

- Never think that Jesus commanded a trifle, nor dare to trifle with anything He has commanded.

Committees

- If there had been a committee appointed, Noah's ark would never have been built.

Complaining

- We are often complaining that our days are few, and yet acting as if there were no end to them!

Consequences

- If a man gets drunk and goes out and breaks his leg so that it must be amputated, God will forgive him if he asks it, but he will have to hop around on one leg all his life.

Creed

- A creed is the road or street. It is very good as far as it goes but if it doesn't take us to Christ it is worthless.

- The man that hasn't any love in his religion, I don't want it; it is human. The man that hasn't any love in his creed may let it go to the winds, I don't want it. "By this shall all men know that ye are my disciples, that you have love one toward another." That is the fruit of the Spirit.

Current

- I thought when I became a Christian I had nothing to do but just to lay my oars in the bottom of the boat and float along. But I soon found that I would have to go against the current.

Curse

- A saint is often under a cross; never under a curse.

Death

- As I go into a cemetery I like to think of the time when the dead shall rise from their graves. Thank God, our friends are not buried; they are only sown.

- While on his deathbed, D.L. Moody cried out: "This is my Coronation Day. Don't try to call me back."

Delegation

- I would rather have ten men to do the work of one man than have one man to do the work of ten.

Division

- I have never yet known the Spirit of God to work where the Lord's people were divided.

Doctors

- Doctors are called devils by the faith healers. Do you ask what I would do if I were ill? Get the best doctor in town, trust in him, and trust in the Lord to work through him.

Doubting

- If you pray for bread and bring no basket to carry it, you prove the doubting spirit, which may be the only hindrance to the boon you ask.

Election

- Do not stumble at the doctrine of election. Preach the Gospel to all; and, as someone has said, if you convert anyone who was not 'chosen,' God will forgive you.

Emptiness

- God sends no-one away empty except they are full of themselves.

Enemies

- The worst enemy one has to overcome, after all, is oneself.

- I tell you I had rather have 10,000 enemies outside than one inside.

Eternal Security

- It is said that D. L. Moody was once accosted on a Chicago street by a drunk who exclaimed, "Aren't you Mr. Moody? Why, I'm one of your converts!" Said Moody in reply, "That must be true, for you surely aren't one of the Lord's."

- The gospel promises not only forgiveness of sins but also new life. When a person receives this new life, his or her life should begin to show some changes.

Evangelism

- If this world is going to be reached, I am convinced that it must be done by men and women of average talent. After all, there are comparatively few people in the world who have great talents.

Example

- A good example is far better than a good precept.

- Where one man reads the Bible, a hundred read you and me.

- A man ought to live so that everybody knows he is a Christian and most of all, his *family* ought to know.

Excuses

- Excuses are the cradle that Satan rocks men off to sleep in.

- It is easy enough to excuse yourself to hell, but you cannot excuse yourself to heaven.

- For six thousand years, making excuses has been Satan's chief business. He is an expert.

Faith

- Faith makes all things possible, love makes all things easy.

- Faith *seems* to be as feeble as a wall of waters; but it is as strong as a wall of iron.

- Strong faith can live in any climate.

- Faith is better than funds for the life that now is, and for the life that is to come.

Family Life

- If Christ is in your house your neighbours will soon know about it.

Fellowship

- You know that some men grow smaller and smaller on an intimate acquaintance; but my experience is that the more and more you know of Christ the larger He becomes.

Fools

- "The fool hath said in his heart, there is no God." The Bible was not written for fools: a wise man knows there is a God, so he need not be told so in the Bible.

Giving

- Give yourself. Money is of very small account in the sight of God.

God

- God writes with a pen that never blots; speaks with a tongue that never slips; and acts with a hand that never fails.

Grace

- I find that many Christians are in trouble about the future; they think they will not have grace enough to live by. It seems to me that death is of very little importance in the meantime. When the dying hour comes, there will be dying grace; but you do not require dying grace to live by.

- God hath assistance for the humble, but resistance for the proud.

- A man can no more take in a supply of grace for the future than he can eat enough for the next six months or take sufficient air into his lungs at one time to sustain life for a week. We must draw upon God's boundless store of grace from day to day as we need it.

- Law tells me how crooked I am. Grace comes along and straightens me out.

Greatness

- The beginning of greatness is to be little; the increase of greatness is to be less; the perfection of greatness is to be nothing.

Happiness

- To be miserable look within;
  To be distracted, look around;
  To be happy, look up.

- God does not call upon us to give up a single thing that adds to our happiness; all He wants us to give up are the things which are the blight of our lives.

Heart

- Without water, clay becomes like stone. Without the grace of God, the heart becomes hard.

Heaven

- It has been said that there will be three things which will surprise us when we get to Heaven; one, to find many whom we did not expect to find there; two, to find some not there whom we had expected; and third, and perhaps the greatest wonder, to find ourselves there!

- This is a land of sin and death and tears - but up yonder is unceasing joy.

- We talk about heaven being so far away. It is within speaking distance to those who belong there. Heaven is a prepared place for a prepared people.

- How far away is heaven? It is not so far as some imagine. It wasn't very far from Daniel. It was not so far off that Elijah's prayer and those of others could not be heard there. Men full of the Spirit can look right into heaven.

Hell

- When we preach on hell, we might at least do it with tears in our eyes.

- Better limp to heaven, than leap to hell.

Holiness

- A holy life will produce the deepest impression. Lighthouses blow no horns; they only shine.

- Holiness is that which the sinner scorns and the Saviour crowns.

Holy Spirit

- There is not a better evangelist in the world than the Holy Spirit.

- God commands us to be filled with the Spirit; and if we aren't filled it's because we're living beneath our privileges.

- If you have been born of the Holy Spirit, you will not *have* to serve God....it will become the natural thing to do.

- I believe firmly that the moment our hearts are emptied of pride and selfishness and ambition and everything that is contrary to

God's law, the Holy Spirit will fill every corner of our hearts. But if we are full of pride and conceit and ambition and the world, there is no room for the Spirit of God.

Home

- If a man had not grace to keep his temper, he is not fit to work for God. If he cannot live uprightly at home, he is not fit for God's service; and the less he does the better. But he *can* keep his temper, he *can* live uprightly at home, by the grace of God.

Humility

- A humble saint looks like a citizen of heaven.

- Humility is to have a just estimate of one's self.

- Give me the homely vessel of humility that God shall preserve and fill with the wine of His grace, rather than the varnished cup of pride which He will dash in pieces like a potter's vessel.

- Be humble or you'll stumble.

Hypocrisy

- Whitewashing the pump won't make the water pure.

Idols

- You don't have to go to heathen lands today to find false gods. America is full of them. Whatever you love more than God is your idol.

Illumination

- The Bible without the Holy Spirit is a sundial by moonlight.

- I remember one night when the Bible was the driest and darkest Book in the universe to me. The next day it was all light. I had the key to it. I had been born of the Spirit. But before I knew anything of the mind of God in His Word I had to give up my sin.

Joy

- The Lord gives His people perpetual joy when they walk in obedience to Him.

- People should look for joy in the Word and not in the world.

- A joy that does not constrain me to go out and work for the Master is purely sentiment and not real joy.

Law

- The law brings out sin; grace covers it. The law wounds; the gospel heals. One is a quiver of arrows; the other a cruse of oil.

Liberty

- The Spirit of God first imparts love; He next inspires hope, and then gives liberty; and that is about the last thing we have in many of our churches.

Life

- Let God have your life; He can do more with it than you can.

Little Things

- Our great matters are little to His power, our little matters are great to His love.

Love

- A man may be a good doctor without loving his patients; a good lawyer without loving his clients; a good geologist without loving science; but he cannot be a good Christian without love.

- I know of no truth in the whole Bible that ought to come home to us with such power and tenderness as that of the love of God.

- God hates sin but He loves the sinner.

- If you can really make a man believe you love him, you have won him; and if I could only make people really believe that God loves them, what a rush we would see for the kingdom of God!

- If we have got the true love of God shed abroad in our hearts, we will show it in our lives. We will not have to go up and down the earth proclaiming it. We will show it in everything we say or do.

Numbers

- Small numbers make no difference to God. There is nothing small if God is in it.

Obedience

- Obedience is the best Commentary on the Bible.

- Sacrifice without obedience is sacrilege.

- Obedience means marching right on whether we feel like it or not. Many times we go against our feelings. Faith is one thing; feeling is another.

- I believe the wretchedness and misery and woe in this country today came from disobedience to God. If they won't obey God as a nation let *us* begin individually.

Old Age

- Old age is a sunset and a sunrise in one. We cannot climb the hills as in youth; but we can mount up as on eagles' wings, if we have found in Christ the secret of eternal life.

Perfection

- The nearer men are to being sinless, the less they talk about it.

- The children of God are not perfect, but we are perfectly His children.

Perseverance

- A child once said to his mother, "You never speak ill of any one. I think you would have something good to say of the Devil." "Well," she said, "imitate his perseverance."

Prayer

- Prayer is a serious thing. We may be taken at our words.

- Men generally pray in public in inverse proportion to their private prayers. If they pray a great deal in private, they are apt to be rather short in public prayer. If they pray very little in private, they are in danger of being more lengthy.

- I have often said I had rather be able to pray like Daniel than to preach like Gabriel.

- We ought to see the face of God every morning before we see the face of man.

- Prayer does not mean that I am to bring God down to my thoughts and my purposes, and bend His government according to my foolish, silly, and sometimes sinful notions. Prayer means that I am to be raised up into feeling, into union and design with Him; that I am to enter into His counsel and carry out His purpose fully.

- If you have so much business to attend to that you have no time to pray, depend upon it that you have more business on hand than God ever intended you should have.

- Some men's prayers need to be cut short at both ends and set on fire in the middle.

- In all thy prayers let thy heart be without the words rather than thy words without the heart.

- We do not hear of long prayers in the Bible except at the dedication of Solomon's Temple and that comes but once in centuries.

Preaching

- Don't you know my friend, it is not the most fluent man that has the greatest effect with a jury? It is the man who tells the truth.

- We might as well have an icicle in the pulpit as a man who leaves Christ out.

- One who can interest children can always interest adults.

- The man who howls about Moody is the one who has been hit. Did you ever notice that when you throw a brick into a bunch of dogs the one who is hit yelps the most, and the others go off about their business?

- We don't want manuscript sermons now. What we want is sermons with our hands and feet.

Pride

- Pride never prepares a man for paradise, but for perdition.

- Pride is the mother of division.

- The worst enemy man has is himself. His pride and self confidence often ruin him. They keep him from trusting to the arms of a loving Saviour.

Profession

- It is wrong for a man or woman to profess what they don't possess.

Promises

- God never made a promise that was too good to be true.

- Unclaimed promises are like uncashed cheques. They will keep you from bankruptcy, but not from want.

- The promises of God are the moulds into which we pour our prayers.

- I challenge any infidel to put his finger on any promise that God has not kept. For 6,000 years the Devil has been trying to find out if God has broken His Word.

Quakers

- (On his not enlisting in the Civil War) There has never been a time in my life when I felt that I could take a gun and shoot down a fellow being. In this respect I am a Quaker.

Repentance

- Man is born with his back toward God. When he truly repents, he turns right around and faces God. Repentance is a change of mind. Repentance is the tear in the eye of faith.

- Prayer before repentance is unavailing. We must put away our sin.

Revival

- The best way to revive a church is to build a fire in the pulpit.

Riches

- Christian men often become rich, but rich men seldom become Christians.

Sabbath

- You show me a nation that has given up the Sabbath and I will show you a nation that has got the seed of decay.

- Men try to rob God of their time by desecrating the Sabbath by toiling; but they die off younger.

Salvation

- Looking at the wound of sin will never save anyone. What you must do is look at the remedy.

- Salvation is worth working for. It is worth a man's going round the world on his hands and knees, climbing its mountains, crossing its valleys, swimming its rivers, going through all manner of hardship in order to attain it. But we do not get it in that way. It is to him who believes.

Sanctification

- God doesn't seek for golden vessels, and does not ask for silver ones, but He must have clean ones.

- Next to the might of God, the serene beauty of a holy life is the most powerful influence for good in all the world.

Satan

- My friends, you are no match for Satan, and when he wants to fight you just run to your elder Brother, who is more than a match for all the devils in hell.

Satisfaction

- The soul that has been satisfied by Christ does not need earth's sweetness.

Sectarianism

- If I thought I had one drop of sectarian blood in my veins, I would let it out before I went to bed; if I had one sectarian hair in my head, I would pull it out.

Self Confidence

- When a man thinks he has got a good deal of strength, and is self confident, you may look for his downfall. It may be years before it comes to light, but it is already commenced.

Self Righteousness

- I have no use for the man who thinks he is so good that he wants a little harp all for himself when he gets to heaven.

Service

- God always uses the man closest to Him.

- The reward of service is more service.

- We may easily be too big for God to use, but never too small.

- The measure of a man is not how many servants he has, but how many men he serves.

- God cannot use you until you are willing to have the world point the finger of scorn at you.

Sin

- When man makes a covenant with sin, he must pay dearly for his pleasure.

- If you commit one sin, it will cause you many sorrows and the world many triumphs.

- He who sins for profit shall not profit by his sins.

- There are two ways of covering our sins: man's way and God's way. If you seek to hide them, they will have a resurrection sometime; but if you let the Lord cover them, neither the Devil nor man will ever be able to find them again.

- There is a great difference between sin dwelling and reigning in us. It dwells in every believer, but reigns in the unbeliever.

- Every sin is a fountain.

Single Mindedness

- Give me a person who says, "This one thing I do, and not these fifty things I dabble in."

Soul

- We know what it is to lose health and wealth and reputation, but what is the loss of all these things compared with the loss of the soul?

Soul Winning

- There is no greater honour than to be the instrument in God's hands of leading one person out of the kingdom of Satan into the glorious light of Heaven.

- The greatest purpose in life is to win souls.

Strength

- When a man has no strength, if he leans on God he becomes powerful.

Success

- You cannot find any place in scripture where a man was ever sent by God to do a work in which he failed.

Tears

- There are no tears in Heaven, and there would be few on earth if the will of God was only done.

Temptation

- There is no one beyond the reach of the tempter. Keep that in mind. Life may run smoothly for awhile, but the testing time is coming.

- Fervency in prayer by the power of the Holy Spirit is a good preservative against thoughts rushing in. Flies never settle on a boiling pot.

- After Jesus had seen the open heavens, Satan tempted Him. The more the blessing, the keener the temptation; for you are worth tempting.

- To be tempted is not to sin. The strongest attacks are made on the strongest forts.

- Temptations are never so dangerous as when they come to us in a religious garb.

Tongue

- His heart cannot be pure whose tongue is not clean.

Trial

- God had one Son without sin, but He never had a Son without trial.

Trouble

- I have more trouble with D. L. Moody than with any other man I ever met.

- There can come upon us no trouble or trial in this life, but God has grace enough to carry us right through it, if we only go to Him and get it. But we must ask for it day by day. "As thy days, so shall thy strength be."

Unbelief

- Unbelief in the heart is like the worm in Jonah's gourd – an unseen adversary.

Unkindness

- Unkindness to the Lord's people, and fellowship with the ungodly, are two great marks of hypocrites.

Walk

- If I walk with the world, I can't walk with God.

- More depends on my walk than talk.

Wealth

- Very few people are satisfied with earthly riches. Often the richer the man the greater the poverty.

- Wealth to most men proves nothing more or less than a great rock upon which their eternity is wrecked.

- He that overcometh shall inherit all things. God has no poor children.

Witnessing

- If we cannot all be lighthouses, any one of us can at any rate be a tallow candle.

- It does not say, "make your light shine," but "let your light shine." You can't make a light shine. If it is really a light it will shine in spite of you – only don't hide it under a bushel. Let it shine. confess Christ everywhere.

Work

- God never lacks a man for his work.

- The more we use the means and opportunities we have, the more will our ability and our opportunities be increased.

- Many people are working and working, like children on a rocking horse – it is a beautiful motion, but there is no progress.

World

- A true Christian loves not the world, yet he loves all the world.

- A man said to me some time ago: "Mr. Moody, now that I am converted, have I to give up the world?"
  "No" said I, "you haven't to give up the world. If you give a good ringing testimony for the Son of God, the world will give you up pretty quick; they won't want you."

- The tendency of the world is down – God's path is up.

- We should be in the world, but the world should not be in us.

- If I walk with the world I can't walk with God.

- If the world cannot tell the difference between us and other men, it is a pretty good sign that we have not been redeemed by the precious blood of Christ.

- Are you going to rule the world, or the world rule you?

Youth

- Youthful sins lay a foundation for aged sorrows.

Zeal

- We are suffering more today from professed Christians, who have either gone to sleep or who have never wakened up, than from any one cause.

- Have zeal, if it is good zeal. I would rather have zeal without knowledge than knowledge without zeal. Don't let these *conservative* men scare you out of your wits. Zeal without knowledge! I pity those men who have great knowledge and no fire back of it.

3

LIVING INSIGHTS
AND ILLUSTRATIONS

DR. WILBUR M. SMITH SAID OF MOODY'S SERMONS:
"NO PREACHER OF THE NINETEENTH CENTURY USED
illustration so frequently and so forcefully as D. L. Moody.
Sometimes two thirds of an entire sermon would consist of a series
of illustrations. Moody himself, reflecting on his homiletical
training, said, "If every minister of the gospel had the same training
as I went through, there would not be such long sermons preached
or so many empty seats. I preached for years in the army and on the
streets, and I learned to say what I had to say rapidly and forcibly,
backing up my points with apt illustrations, just as Christ enforced
his sayings with striking parables. This is the way to keep an
audience interested." Once he overheard two people walking home

in the dark after one of his meetings. "Did Moody preach tonight?" one asked.

The other replied, "No, he didn't; he only talked." That comment reflected Moody's natural style: "If I can only get people to think I am talking with them, and not preaching," he said, "it is so much easier to get their attention."

Some of the following are illustrations used by Moody himself and others are incidents related by individuals who have met him.

•••

I am sometimes startled at the ease with which a soul can be won, and I'm often humiliated when I think of the many opportunities I have wasted.

Not long ago, when a hackman got down to open the door for me, I dropped him a quarter, grasped his hand, and said, "Goodnight. I hope to meet you in glory."

I had often done that and thought nothing of it in this case. I went into the house, met my host, and retired for the night. About midnight, my host knocked at my chamber door.

"Chaplain," he said, "that hackman has come back. He says he has got to see you tonight. I told him he better wait until morning, but he said, 'No, sir, I must see him tonight, and I know he will be willing to see me.'"

A broad shouldered, rough looking man with a great whip in his hand, the hackman stood in my presence. Tears rolled down his cheeks like rain.

"If I'm to meet you in glory, I have got to turn around," he said. "I have come to ask you to pray with me."

What a privilege it was to pray with that man and to point him to Jesus! And yet, I had never seen him before in all my life. Thousands of men and women in the country have not had an invitation to come to God in all their lives.

•••

Moody was once asked, "How many converts did you have last night?" He answered, "Two and one-half."

"You mean two adults and one child?"

"No," he replied, "Two children and one adult."

A child converted is an entire life converted.

•••

After one of his great evangelistic campaigns in Britain, Mr. Moody sailed for America. A few days at sea, and the ship's shaft had broken and it was sinking. "I was passing," he says, "through a new experience. I had thought myself superior to the fear of death. I had often preached on the subject, and urged Christians to realise this victory of faith. During the Civil War, I had been under fire without fear, I was in Chicago during the great cholera epidemic, and went round with the doctors visiting the sick and dying; where they could go to look after the bodies of men, I said I could go to look after their souls. I remember a case of smallpox where the sufferer's condition was beyond description; yet I went to the bedside of that poor sufferer again and again, with Bible and prayer, for Jesus' sake. In all this I had no fear. But on the sinking ship it was different. There was no cloud between my soul and my Saviour. I knew my sins had been put away, and if I died there it would only be to wake up in heaven. That was all settled long ago. But as my thoughts went out to my beloved ones at home – my wife, my children, my friends on both sides of the sea, the schools and all the interests so dear to me – and as I realised that perhaps the next hour would separate me forever from all these, so far as this world was concerned, I confess it almost broke me down. It was the darkest hour of my life."

•••

Some say that faith is the gift of God. So is the air, but you have to breathe it; so is bread, but you have to eat it. Some are wanting a miraculous kind of feeling. That is not faith.

"Faith cometh by hearing and hearing by the Word of God." (Rom.10: 17). That is whence faith comes. It is not for me to sit down and wait for faith to come stealing over me with a strong sensation, but is for me to take God at His Word."

•••

A President's Recollection
(As recalled by President Woodrow Wilson)

I was sitting in a barbershop chair when I became aware that a personality had entered the room. A man had quietly come in upon the same errand as myself and sat in the chair next to me. Every word he uttered, though not in the least didactic, showed a personal and vital interest in the man who was serving him. And before I got through, I was aware that I had attended an evangelistic service. Mr. Moody was in the next chair. I purposely lingered after he left and noted the singular effect his visit had upon the barbers in that shop. They talked in undertones. They did not know his name, but they knew that something had elevated their thought. And I felt that I left that place as I should have left a place of worship.

•••

Some years ago a gentleman asked me which I thought was the most precious promise of all those that Christ left. I took some time to look over the promises, but I gave it up. I found that I could not answer the question. Like a man with a large family of children, he cannot tell which he likes best because he loves them all.

•••

I sometimes tremble when I hear people quote promises, and say that God is bound to fulfil those promises to them, when all the time there is some sin in their lives they are not willing to give up. It is well for us to search our hearts, and find out why it is that our prayers are not answered.

•••

On a special evening meeting held in a London suburb, Mr. Moody spoke on John 3:16, emphasising the freeness of God's unspeakable gift. He held up his large marked Bible and told how much he valued it, but that he would give it as a gift to the first one who took him at his word. The huge hall was densely packed. A large number of soldiers occupied the middle of the building in front of the platform, their scarlet uniforms making them conspicuous. As Moody stood with his treasured Bible in his hand offering it to whoever would take it, a soldier sprang forward and grasped it from Mr. Moody's hand. "I'll have it!" he said, and returned to his seat clutching his precious gift.

A sound swept through the large audience like the wind over a field of ripe corn. Everyone seemed to be saying, "Oh, if I had only known he meant it. Oh, if only I had taken it."

Then Mr. Moody quoted, "I will give unto him that is athirst of the fountain of the water of life freely" (Rev. 21:6) "whosoever will, let him take the water of life freely" (22:17). Many of the audience made their way to the inquiry room afterwards, and many indeed received of the water of life freely.

•••

Once I found a little girl on one of Chicago's sidewalks and invited her to my mission school. But the ragged child would not promise to attend. I persisted, telling of the good times they had, the singing, and the candy, but she only shook her head. I pressed further until she finally promised to come. Sunday came, and she did not show up.

Out into the street I went to search for the child. My eye fell on her about the same time as hers fell on me. Off she dashed in a mad rush for home, Undaunted, I took off after her until she disappeared between the swinging doors of a saloon.

I continued the pursuit, and she led me out the back door, up the steps to her tenement flat, into her bedroom, and under the bed. And there, breathing hard, I finally caught up with her.

At that moment the girl's mother appeared and angrily demanded to know who the intruder was. I introduced myself, and explained my purpose, and won for the mission school not only the girl, but also her brothers and sisters.

•••

There was a shop girl in Chicago a few years ago; one day she could not have bought a dollar's worth of anything; the next day she could buy a thousand dollars worth of everything she wanted. What made the difference? She married a rich husband. She had accepted him and, of course, all he had became hers. And so you can have everything, if only you will receive Christ.

•••

After one of Moody's meetings, a locomotive engineer came forward and said he had decided to become a missionary to a foreign country. Moody asked him if his fireman were a Christian, "I don't know," was the reply, "I never asked him."

"Well," said Moody, "why don't you start with your fireman?"

•••

D. L. Moody called it the biggest blunder of his life. It happened on October 8, 1871, during a preaching series in Farwell Hall, Chicago. His text was "What shall I do then with Jesus which is called Christ?" (Matt. 27:22). At the conclusion of the sermon Moody said he would give the people one week to make up their minds about Jesus. He then turned to Ira Sankey for a solo, and Sankey sang "Today the Saviour Calls."

But by the third verse Sankey's voice was drowned out by the noise outside the hall. The great Chicago fire had begun, and the flames were even then sweeping toward the Hall. The clanging of the fire bells and the noise of the engines made it impossible to continue the meeting.

In the years that followed, Moody wished that he had called for an immediate decision for Christ.

•••

After the great Chicago Fire, a friend approached D. L. Moody and said, "I hear you lost everything."

"Well, you understand it wrong," the evangelist replied.

"How much have you left?"

"I can't tell you; I have a good deal more left than I lost," said Moody.

"You can't tell how much you have?" the man asked.

"No."

"I didn't know you were ever that rich."

"I suppose you didn't!"

"What do you mean?" the perplexed friend inquired.

Moody opened his Bible to Revelation 21:7: "He that overcometh shall inherit all things; and I will be his God."

•••

After the Chicago fire, D. L. Moody went to the East Coast to rest and reflect. He felt a sterility in his ministry and needed a new touch from God. While he was conducting Bible readings in Brooklyn, an event took place that led to one of the great spiritual experiences in Moody's life.

Douglas Russell, a British evangelist friend, visited the meetings and gave a study on Galatians 4. He pointed out that whereas all Christians were born of the Spirit, not all Christians were filled with the Spirit. The thought struck Moody, who said, "I never saw that before! Been troubled about that for years."

The next day, Moody was walking down Wall Street, meditating on this truth, when God met him in a special way. Moody said:

"Oh, what a day! I cannot describe it; I seldom refer to it; it is almost too sacred an experience to name. I can only say that God revealed Himself to me, and I had such an experience of His love that I had to ask Him to stay His hand."

The new power that came to the evangelist lit a flame in the meetings, and more than one hundred sinners found Christ.

It was in 1873, in Dublin, that D. L. Moody heard British evangelist Henry Varley utter those life-changing words: "The world has yet to see what God can do with and for and through and in a man who is fully and wholly consecrated to Him."

It was after an all-night prayer meeting, at the home of Henry Bewley. Varley did not even remember making the statement when Moody reminded him of it a year later.

" As I crossed the wide Atlantic," Moody said, "the boards of the deck were engraved with them, and when I reached Chicago, the very paving stones seemed marked with them." The result: Moody decided he was involved in too many ministries to be effective and therefore began to concentrate on evangelism.

•••

After the 1873 Glasgow campaign, D. L. Moody and Ira Sankey took the train to Edinburgh for a three-day meeting. Sankey was reading the paper, looking for some news from America; but all he found that interested him was a religious poem in the corner of a page of advertising. The words were written by a frail Scottish lady, Elizabeth C. Clephane, who lived near Edinburgh. He read it to

Moody who, absorbed in a letter from home, heard nothing. He was so impressed with the words that he put the clipping in his pocket

At the noon meeting a day or two later Moody spoke on "The Good Shepherd," and then asked Sankey to close with an appropriate song. All the singer could think of was the poem on the parable of the lost sheep, so he put the newspaper clipping on the organ, lifted a silent prayer, struck an A-flat, and began to sing for the first time 'The Ninety and Nine.'

"Note by note the tune was given," Sankey wrote in later years. "As the singing ceased a great sigh seemed to go up from the meeting, and I knew that the song had reached the hearts of my Scottish audience."

Moody was greatly stirred by the song and asked Sankey where he had found it. "I never heard the like of it in my life!" he said. Sankey explained that it was the poem he had read to Moody from the newspaper during their train ride.

•••

On October 19, just a few weeks before Moody and Sankey arrived in Edinburgh for a campaign, the leading 'spiritual giant' of Scotland, Dr. R. S. Candlish, died. Before he died, he predicted that there would come to Scotland 'a great blessing which should not be despised, though it come strangely.' Moody and Sankey were the 'strange' bearers of that blessing.

•••

D. L. Moody was never ordained. He was a layman who was wholly yielded to Christ, and preaching and winning souls was "important business" to him. Those who have analysed his preaching tell us that his sermons averaged about half-an-hour in length. He used short sentences, averaging about seventeen words, and short words, 80 percent of them monosyllables. He used few adjectives and adverbs, but majored on verbs with a lot of action. He used the language of the marketplace and sought to reach the common man.

"We have too many orators," he said. "I am tired and sick of your 'silver-tongued orators.' I used to mourn because I couldn't be an orator. I thought, *Oh, if I could only have the gift of speech like some men.*"

•••

It was in 1875, during Moody's great British campaign, that former Prime Minister William Gladstone took Matthew Arnold, the famous writer and critic, to hear D. L. Moody preach. After the meeting, Gladstone said: "I thank God that I have lived to see the day when He should bless His church on earth by the gift of a man able to preach the Gospel of Christ as we have heard it preached this afternoon!"

The intellectual Arnold replied, "Mr. Gladstone, I would give all I possess if I could only believe it!"

•••

In 1884 D. L. Moody returned to Britain, and one day was involved with the famous cricketer C. T. Studd in a meeting at a theatre. A young London intern was attracted to the meeting, but when he walked in he found that a man was leading in prayer and apparently never going to finish it. But as the young doctor arose to leave, he heard an American voice say, "Let us sing a hymn while our brother finishes his prayer!" It was Moody. The doctor was so impressed that he stayed for the rest of the service and then returned for another meeting. As a result, the doctor, Wilfred Grenfell, gave his heart and life to Christ, and his missionary work in Labrador earned him knighthood from King George V.

•••

One of the special features of the 1893 Columbian Exposition in Chicago was the Parliament of Religions. D. L. Moody decided that he would use the world's fair and the parliament as an opportunity to proclaim Christ. His more conservative friends criticized him for "joining" with other religions, especially those that denied Christ; but Moody was persistent.

"I am not going to attack it," Moody explained. "I am going to make Jesus Christ so attractive that men will turn to Him."

His one concern was to reach the lost, and he would not allow man-made barriers to hinder him. He said: "I'll preach Christ crucified anywhere I can find lost men, on the street, in the open air, in tents or in saloons, in beer gardens or in missions, in theatres or halls, in churches or in the Parliament of Religions."

•••

At Northfield, Massachusetts, D. L. Moody founded several schools for the training of underprivileged children. Whenever students arrived at the train station, if Moody was in town, he would take his buggy and meet them. One rainy day a man and two women arrived at the station and looked around for someone to take them to the hotel. Seeing a man in a buggy, the visitor insisted that he drive them to the hotel. "I'm waiting for some seminary girls," Moody explained. The visitor was offended. "These girls are not the only people to be served!" he said. "Now, you just take us right up to the hotel!"

Meekly the driver obeyed, left them at the hotel, and drove off before he could be paid.

"Who was that driver?" the visitor asked the bellboy. "Mr. D. L. Moody," the boy replied.

The visitor was shocked, because he was at Northfield to ask Moody to take his daughter into the school. The next day the man apologized, and Moody had a great deal of fun over it.

•••

A man once testified in one of D. L. Moody's meetings that he had lived "on the Mount of Transfiguration" for five years.

"How many souls did you lead to Christ last year?" Moody bluntly asked him.

"Well," the man hesitated, "I don't know."

"Have you saved any?" Moody persisted.

"I don't know that I have," the man admitted.

"Well," said Moody, "we don't want that kind of mountaintop experience. When a man gets up so high that he cannot reach down and save poor sinners, there is something wrong."

•••

The children that D. L. Moody recruited for his Chicago Sunday school were among some of the worst characters in the city, boys with nicknames like "Red Eye," "Madden the Butcher," "Rag Breeches Cadet," and the ringleader of the gang, "Butcher" Kilroy. Moody never condescended to them, always treated them with firmness and love, and sought to win them to Christ. When "Butcher" Kilroy first attended the school, he was dressed like a beggar: a man's old overcoat around his body, papers around his legs, and a big pair of shoes on his feet. Moody treated him as though he were the best-dressed child in the school. The gang of rough boys was known as "Moody's Bodyguard." He promised them each a new suit if they faithfully attended Sunday school, and twelve of the fourteen boys earned their suits.

Moody had a photographer take "before and after" shots, which were labelled: "Will it pay?" and "It does pay!"

•••

A man named Stillson was one of D. L. Moody's assistants in his Sunday school ministry in Chicago. Stillson noted that Moody was not really preparing his Sunday school addresses. He would have prayer with the leaders, choose a Bible verse "to depart from," and tell stories from his previous week's experiences in   witnessing and visiting.

"Moody," Stillson told him one day, "if you want to draw wine out of a cask put some in. You are all the time talking, and you ought to begin to study."

Stillson lined up some books for Moody to read, but when Stillson left Chicago and returned to his Rochester, New York home, the training process ceased. Moody was a great learner, but he learned more from life than from books.

•••

While making a visit in a home, D. L. Moody persuaded the wife to get rid of her husband's whiskey. In fact, Moody emptied the jug in the street! When he returned the next afternoon to take the children to North Market Mission Hall, he found himself confronting several irate men who threatened to beat him.

"See here now, my men," said Moody, "if you are going to whip me for spilling the whiskey, you might at least give me time to say my prayers." The men thought that his praying would just add more fun to the event, so Moody knelt down to pray. He prayed as they had never heard a man pray before, and the longer he prayed, the more their hearts softened. When he arose from his knees, he found the men giving him their hands and saying that he was not such a bad fellow after all! Safely delivered, Moody was soon marching the children to the mission!

•••

One of D. L. Moody's Sunday school teachers was absent one Sunday, and Moody visited him to discover the problem.

The man explained that his doctor had told him he had but a short time to live because he was bleeding in his lungs, and he was planning to go home to his widowed mother to die. However, his great concern was not himself, but rather the spiritual condition of the children in his class.

Moody offered to go with the man to visit each child. In spite of his physical weakness, the teacher would call on each pupil and then with tears implore him to come to Christ. At the close of ten days of visiting, Moody and the teacher saw the last child yield to Christ. The entire class, now born again, met at the railroad station to see the dying teacher off the next day.

Moody called the experience "the most memorable I have ever known," because it increased his personal concern for lost souls.

•••

While greeting people as they left the evening service at North Market Hall, Moody was approached by a man who deliberately insulted him. Moody pushed the man away only to send him tumbling down the stairs to the lower vestibule.

When Moody went to the platform to start the second service, he said: "Friends, before beginning tonight, I want to confess that I yielded just now to my temper, out in the hall, and I have done wrong. If that man is present here, I want to ask his forgiveness, and God's. Let us pray."

•••

D. L. Moody's businesslike, New England honesty showed up in strange ways.

A man who was a constant troublemaker in Moody's Chicago ministry approached the evangelist to shake his hand. Moody hesitated, and then shook the man's hand, saying to him, "I suppose

if Jesus Christ could eat the Last Supper with Judas Iscariot, I ought
to shake hands with you."

•••

D. L. Moody was never afraid to do something new or to risk
ridicule from people, even other Christians.

"There's a class:" he said, "very much afraid of being called
'peculiar.' They hesitate to work for Christ because they will be
considered peculiar. You will notice that when God has some work
to do, He generally calls peculiar people to do it."

In Chicago, Moody was called "Crazy Moody." Even the
newspapers printed stories and jokes about him.

•••

D. L. Moody made a covenant with God that he would witness
for Christ to at least one person each day. One night, about ten o'clock,
he realized that he had not yet witnessed; so he went out into the
street and spoke to a man standing by a lamppost, asking him, " Are
you a Christian?"

The man flew into a violent rage and threatened to knock Moody
into the gutter. Later, that same man went to an elder in the church
and complained that Moody was "doing more harm in Chicago than
ten men were doing good." The elder begged Moody to temper his
zeal with knowledge.

Three months later, Moody was awakened at the YMCA by a
man knocking at the door. It was the man he had witnessed to.
"I want to talk to you about my soul," he said to Moody. He
apologized for the way he had treated Moody and said that he had
had no peace ever since that night on Lake Street when Moody
witnessed to him. Moody led the man to Christ and he became a
zealous worker in the Sunday school.

•••

On April 25, 1855, Edward Kimball led young Dwight L. Moody to faith in Christ in the back of Samuel Holton's shoe store in Boston where Moody was employed. (Holton was Moody's uncle.)

Kimball was Moody's Sunday school teacher at the Mount Vernon Church and he said, "I have seen few persons whose minds were spiritually darker than his was when he came into my class."

Kimball admitted that he himself was hesitant about approaching young Moody concerning his soul. He walked past the store, stopped, and then "determined to make a dash for it and have it over at once." The Spirit was working, Moody was ready and he trusted Christ.

"I was in a new world," Moody said in later years when he told the story of his conversion. "The next morning the sun shone brighter and the birds sang sweeter, the old elms waved their branches for joy, and all Nature was at peace. It was the most delicious joy that I'd ever known."

•••

Young D. L. Moody did not have an easy time becoming a member of the Mount Vernon Church in Boston. He knew he was converted, but he was unable to express his thoughts the way the seasoned saints expected. So zealous was he in the witnessing of his faith that one of the deacons took him aside and said, "Young man, you can serve the Lord better by keeping still."

Edward Kimball, who had led Moody to Christ, said that the membership committee had seldom met an applicant for membership who was more unlikely to be a good member and a useful worker than D. L. Moody. How wrong they were! After a year of special preparation, Moody was finally admitted into the membership of the church.

•••

D. L. Moody was quite frank with people when they spoke publicly and were out of line. After a prayer meeting, Moody said to a man, "You ought not to have said what you did tonight, and besides, your record is all bad, and you ought not to take part at all."

"Sir, you hurt my feelings," the man replied.

"Well," Moody returned, "you hurt mine. I have feelings as well as you, and you hurt the feelings of five hundred other people besides."

•••

Mr. and Mrs. Moody often had guests in their Chicago home. One evening, after a very demanding day, Moody asked a visiting Christian to lead in family devotions. The man waxed eloquent as he expounded the symbolism in a difficult chapter of the Bible. Then he prayed at great length. When the worship was over, Mrs. Moody and the guest got up from their knees, but Moody remained bowed in prayer. The guest thought that he was praying, but Mrs. Moody soon detected that her husband was asleep.

•••

One New Year's day, Moody took the deacons of his Illinois Street Independent Church on a marathon visitation ministry. They made 200 calls in one day! The problem was that the deacons could not keep up with Moody; and many of them "fell aside" as the day progressed.

Moody would rush up the stairs to an apartment and introduce himself and the deacons with him. Then he would quickly inquire of the family's spiritual state and whatever material needs they had. He would then pray for the family and be off to the next house. The entire visit would consume less than two minutes.

Moody believed in keeping in contact with his people. One day, he made five visits and reported, "In every home I found a broken heart."

•••

D. L. Moody received an invitation to attend the grand opening of a "magnificent pool hall" on the west side of Chicago. Before the opening, Moody called on the owners to see if he could bring a friend with him. Sceptical of Moody, the partners wanted to know who his "friend" was, but he refused to name him. "Well, I'll ask him to forgive you."

"We don't want any praying" the men replied.

"You've given me an invitation, and I am coming," said Moody.

The men tried to argue with Moody, but he would not give in. Finally, he suggested that perhaps he should pray right then and there. Anxious to get rid of their problem, the partners agreed. Moody went to his knees and asked God to "bless their souls and break their business to pieces."

Within a few months, their business was on the rocks.

•••

At a meeting of the London (England) Sunday School Union, the vice-chairman introduced D. L. Moody as "their American cousin, the Rev. Mr. Moody of Chicago."

Moody responded by saying: "The vice-chairman has made two mistakes. To begin with, I'm not 'the Reverend' Mr. Moody at all. I'm plain Dwight L. Moody, a Sabbath school worker. And then I'm not your 'American cousin.' By the grace of God I'm your brother who is interested with you in our Father's work for His children."

•••

D. L. Moody not only won sinners to Christ, but he won Christians for service. He was travelling through rural Indiana with another Christian layman, and they passed a schoolhouse. "Do they ever hold religious meetings in that schoolhouse?" he asked a woman whose house was next door. She said that there had been no meetings there.

"Well, tell all your neighbours there will be prayer meetings in that schoolhouse every night next week!" Moody said.

Then Moody contacted the teacher of the school and asked that the announcement be sent home with all of the students. Moody's friend knew that Moody was booked up for that entire week, so he casually asked, "Who is going to conduct these meetings?" "You are!" Moody replied.

"I?" the man responded, aghast. "I never did such a thing in my life!"

"It's time you had, then," said the evangelist. "I have made the appointment, and you will have to keep it."

The man did, and the result was another moving of *God* that brought souls to Christ.

•••

D. L. Moody first met Ira Sankey at a YMCA convention in Indianapolis in June 1870. It was at a prayer meeting in a Baptist church at six in the morning. Sankey had arrived late and discovered a man was leading in an interminable prayer. A friend whispered to Sankey, "The singing here has been abominable. I wish you would start up something when that man stops praying - if he ever does."

The man finally stopped and immediately Sankey started singing "There Is A Fountain Filled with Blood." The rest of the crowd, relieved at a new voice and a change of pace, enthusiastically joined in. Afterward, the friend introduced Sankey to Moody who immediately asked him a number of personal questions about himself, his job, his family, and his work.

Moody then announced that Sankey would have to give up his job to come to Chicago and help him in his ministry!

Sankey argued. After all, he had a job, a wife and two small children, and was working for the government. He could not come.

"You must," Moody replied. "I have been looking for you for the last eight years." The next day, Sankey got word that Moody wanted to meet him at a certain street corner at six that evening. When Sankey arrived, Moody put him on a soap box and told him to sing. The song gathered a large crowd of working men and gave Moody a congregation for the preaching of the gospel.

•••

It was the converted English ex-prizefighter, Harry Moorehouse, who taught Moody to preach *from* the Bible, not *about* the Bible, and to emphasize the love of God to sinners. Moody had met Moorehouse in Dublin and casually invited him to preach at his church, should he ever be in Chicago. One day, Moody received word that Moorehouse was on his way! He arranged for him to preach (Moody was to be out of the city anyway), and when Moody returned, he discovered that the young evangelist was making a great impact on the people. He had used the same text (John 3:16) for every sermon!

Rather sceptical, Moody went to the meetings and saw that the church was packed and the people were carrying Bibles. Moorehouse told them to bring their Bibles so they could check up on the preacher! He announced John 3:16 as his text, and then led the people through the Bible, from Genesis to Revelation, and showed them the love of God for sinners.

Moody called this experience his "second conversion." Up to then, he had preached God's hatred for sinners and His terrible wrath; but now he saw that his message was "God is love." "This heart of mine began to thaw out," he said. "I could not hold back the tears." Using his concordance, he studied *love* in the Bible. (Moorehouse also taught him topical Bible study and introduced him to *Cruden's Concordance.)* "I got full of it. It ran out my fingers," Moody said. He decided to stop trying to frighten men into the kingdom of God, but instead to woo them with God's love.

•••

"Some day," D.L. Moody used to say, "you will read in the papers that D. L. Moody of East Northfield is dead. Don 't believe a word of it! At that moment I shall be more alive than I am now!"

His last sermon, which he preached in Kansas City on November 23, 1899, was on the subject "excuses", for which he took as his text the words of Luke 14:18, 'And they all with one consent began to make excuse.' He ended his sermon with an urgent and characteristic appeal for immediate decisions for Christ. "Be wise tonight and accept the invitation! Make up your mind that you will not go away till the question of eternity is settled!"

When he gave the invitation, fifty stood to their feet and went across the street into the inquiry room.

He was too ill to continue the Kansas City campaign, so he took the train back to Northfield. On Friday, December 22, he went "home."

Five years before his homegoing Moody had said, "If it can be said, faithfully said, over my grave, 'Moody has done what he could,' that will be the most glorious epitaph." Instead, I John 2:17 was chosen: "He that doeth the will of God abideth for ever."

•••

In the north of London lived two sisters, the one in health, the other bedridden. As she was one day bemoaning her condition, the thought came to the invalid that she could at least pray. Accordingly, though in perpetual pain, she was yet in constant prayer, crying to God for revival to the church of which she was a member, but which she was unable to attend. Reading in "The Revival" of Moody's work in Chicago, she put the paper under her pillow and began to pray that God would send that man to her church.

When, in 1872, Moody came to England on a brief visit, he had purposed to refrain from preaching. He yielded, however, to the request of Mr. Lessey, and preached one Sunday morning in his church. "Who do you think preached in Church this morning?" said the one sister to the other, on reaching home. Several likely names were suggested. At length she informed her that it was Mr. Moody, from America. "I know what that means," cried the sick woman; "God has answered my prayers." After the evening service of that same day, Mr. Moody made his appeal, and hundreds rose in decision for Christ. He continued there for ten days, during which time four hundred converts were added to that church. Recounting the story, Mr. Moody said: "I wanted to know what this meant. I began making enquiries and never rested until I had found a bedridden girl praying that God would bring me to that church. He had heard her, and brought me over four thousand miles of land and sea in answer to her request."

And now let Dr. Campbell Morgan continue the story. "That girl," he writes, "was a member of my church when I was pastor at New Court, London. She is still a member, still suffering, still confined to her room. When in 1901 I was leaving England for America, I went to see her. She said to me, 'I want you to reach that birthday book.' I did so, and turning to February 5th I saw in the handwriting I knew so well - D. L. Moody, Psa. 91. Then Marianne Adlard said to me, "He wrote that for me when he came to see me in 1872, and I prayed for him every day till he went Home to God." Continuing, she said, "Now will you write your name on your birthday page and let me pray for you until either you or I go Home." I shall never forget writing my name in that book. To me the room was full of the Presence. I have often thought of that hour in the rush of busy life, in the place of toil and strain, and even yet, by God's good grace, I know that Marianne Adlard is praying for me."

•••

Dr. Cuyler, pastor of Lafayette Avenue Presbyterian Church in Brooklyn, New York, made a forceful comparison between Moody and Abraham Lincoln, thus: "Lincoln and Moody possessed alike the gift of an infallible commonsense. Neither of them ever committed a serious mistake. They were alike in being masters of the simple, strong, Saxon speech, the language of the people and of Bunyan, the language that is equal to the loftiest forensic of pulpit eloquence. Lincoln's huge, loving heart gushed out in sympathy for all sorts and conditions of men, and made him the best loved man in America's history. And Moody's big, loving heart, fired with the love of Jesus, made him a master of pathos that touched the fount of tears in thousands of hearts, and often brought weeping multitudes before his pulpit. Finally, Lincoln, the liberator, went up to his martyr crown carrying four millions of shattered manacles in his hands. Moody, the liberator of immortal souls from the fetters of sin, fell the other day a martyr to overwhelming work, and went up to be greeted at the gates of glory by thousands whom he had led from the Cross to the Crown."

•••

Canon W. M. Hay Aitken relates how he was present at a meeting of clergymen, ministers, and laymen in the Freemasons' Hall in 1875 to hear a statement from Mr. Moody regarding the aims and objects of his London mission. One questioner suggested the printing and circulation of a leaflet specifying the doctrines he proposed to expound in his meetings. Moody's reply came swift and decisive: "It has all been printed already; you will find it in the fifty-third chapter of Isaiah." As Aitken left the hall in company with the late Principal Chalmers, the latter whispered with obvious application to the evangelist of the words of Isaiah 41:15, "A sharp threshing instrument, having teeth."

•••

Moody was introduced one day to a religious leader called Bewley in Dublin. "Is this young man O and O?" asked Bewley.

"What do you mean by O and O?" inquired Moody's friend.

"Is he Out and Out for Christ?" was the reply, and Moody never forgot it. Frequently he would talk about being "O and O."

•••

A couple of clowns performing at a Dublin circus tried to ridicule the evangelists with this routine:

"I'm rather Moody tonight, How do you feel?"

"I feel rather Sankeymonious."

The audience began to hiss the so-called comedians and then began to sing 'Hold the Fort.'

•••

When Moody was preaching in Denver, a young lad wanted to hear the evangelist but could not get into the building. "I'll get you in!" said a heavyset man at the back door. "Just hold on to my coat tail." The man was D. L. Moody, and the boy was Paul Rader, who grew up to become one of America's greatest preachers and also a pastor of the Moody Church (1915-21).

•••

Introduced to a colourful elderly evangelist called 'Uncle Johnnie' Vasser, who exclaimed "How glad I am to see the man that

God has used to win so many souls to Christ", Moody replied: "You say rightly, Uncle John, the man whom *God* has *used*"; and stooping to pick up a handful of earth he poured it through his fingers: "There's nothing more than *that* to D. L. Moody, except as God uses him!"

•••

Once in a train with the singer, D. B. Towner, a drunk having a badly bruised eye recognised Moody and started bawling hymns. "Let's get out of here," Moody said, but Towner knew the other cars were full. When the conductor came along Moody pointed out the drunk. The conductor quietly took the fellow, bathed and bandaged his eye and sent him back to the car, where he fell asleep.

"Towner," said Moody after a while, "that is an awful rebuke for me! I preached last night to that crowd against pharisaism and exhorted them to imitate the Good Samaritan, and now this morning God has given me an opportunity to practice what I preached and I find I have both feet in the shoes of the priest and Levite." For the rest of that tour he told the story publicly against himself.

7

4

THE FINEST OF THE WHEAT
EXCERPTS FROM MOODY'S SERMONS

THE MOST PRECIOUS PROMISE

Some years ago a gentleman came to me and asked me which I thought was the most precious promise of all those that Christ left. I took some time to look them over; but I gave it up. I found that I could not answer the question. It is like a man with a large family of children, he cannot tell which he likes best; he loves them all. But if not the best, this is one of the sweetest promises of all; *"Come unto me, all ye that labour and are heavy laden, and I will give you rest. Take my yoke upon you, and learn of me, for I am meek and lowly of heart: and ye shall find rest unto your souls. For my yoke is easy, and my burden is light."*

There are a good many people who think the promises are not going to be fulfilled. There are some that you do see fulfilled, and you cannot help but believe they are true. Now remember, that all the promises are not given without conditions. Some are given with, and others without, conditions attached to them. For instance, we read, "If I regard iniquity in my heart, the Lord will not hear me." Now, I need not pray as long as I am cherishing some known sin. He will not hear me much less answer me. The Lord says in the eighty-fourth Psalm, "No good thing will He withhold from them that walk uprightly." If I am not walking uprightly I have no claims under the promise. Again, some of the promises were made to certain individuals or nations. For instance, God said that He would make Abraham's seed to multiply as the stars of heaven: but that is not a promise for you or me. Some promises were made to the Jews, and do not apply to the Gentiles.

Then there are promises without conditions. He promised Adam and Eve that the world should have a Saviour; and there was no power in earth or perdition that could keep Christ from coming at the appointed time. When Christ left the world, He said He would send us the Holy Ghost. He had only been gone ten days when the Holy Ghost came. And so you can run right through the Scriptures, and you will find that some of the promises are with, and some without, conditions; and if we do not comply with the conditions, we cannot expect them to be fulfilled.

I believe it will be the experience of every man and woman on the face of the earth, I believe that every one will be obliged to testify in the evening of life, that if they have complied with the condition, the Lord has fulfilled his word to the letter. Joshua, the old Hebrew hero, was an illustration. After having tested God forty years in the Egyptian brick-kilns, forty years in the desert, and thirty years in the Promised Land, his dying testimony was: "Not one thing hath failed of all the good things which the Lord promised." I believe you could heave the ocean easier than break one of God's promises. So when we come to a promise like the one we have before us now, I want you to bear in mind that there is no discount upon it. "Come unto me, all ye that labour and are heavy laden, and I will give you rest."

THE FRIEND OF THE SORROW
Luke 4:18 *"He hath sent me to heal the brokenhearted."*

I want to take up this one thought - that Christ was sent into the world to heal the brokenhearted. When the Prince of Wales came to this country a few years ago, the whole country was excited as to his purpose. What was his object in coming here? Had he come to look into our republican form of government, or our institutions, or was it simply to see and be seen? He came and he went without telling us what he came for. When the Prince of Peace came into this dark world He did not come in any private way. He tells us that He came not to see and be seen, but to "seek and to save that which was lost," and also "to heal the brokenhearted." And in the face of this announcement it is a mystery to me why those who have broken hearts will rather carry them year in and year out than just bring them to the great Physician. How many men in Chicago are just going down to their graves with a broken heart? They have carried their hearts weighted with trouble for years and years, and yet when they open the Scriptures they can see the passage telling us that He came here for the purpose of healing the brokenhearted. He left Heaven and all its glory to come to the world - sent by the Father, He tells us, for the purpose of healing the brokenhearted.

You will find, my friends, that there is no class of people exempt from broken hearts. The rich and the poor suffer alike. There was a time, when I used to visit the poor, that I thought all the broken hearts were to be found among them; but within the last few years I have found there are as many broken hearts among the learned as the unlearned, the cultured as the uncultured, the rich as the poor. If you could but go up one of our avenues and down another and reach the hearts of the people, and get them to tell you their whole story, you would be astonished at the wonderful history of every family.

Let me call your attention to this little word 'sent' - "He hath *sent* me." Take your Bibles and read about those who have been sent by God, and one thought will come to you - that no man who has ever been sent by God to do His work has ever failed. No matter how great the work, how mighty the undertaking, no matter how many difficulties had to be encountered, when they were sent from God they were sure to succeed. God sent Moses down to Egypt to bring three million people out of bondage. The idea would have seemed absurd to most people. Fancy a man with an impediment in his speech, without an army, without generals, with no record, bringing three million people from the power of a great nation like that of the Egyptians. But God sent him, and what was the result? Pharaoh said they should not go, and the great king and all his army were going to prevent them. But did he succeed? God sent Moses and he didn't fail. We find that God sent Joshua to the walls of Jericho, and he marched around the walls, and at the proper time these walls came tumbling down and the city fell into his hands. God sent Elijah to stand before Ahab, and we read the result. Samson and Gideon were sent by God, and we are told in the Scriptures what they accomplished; and so all through the Word we find that when God sent men they have never failed. Now, do you think for a moment that God's own Son, sent to us, is going to fail? Do you think if He has come to heal broken hearts, He is going to fail?

Do you think there is a heart so bruised and broken that can't be healed by Him? He can heal them all, but the great trouble is that men won't come. If there is a broken heart here tonight just bring it to the Great Physician. If you break an arm or a leg, you run off and get the best physician. If you have a broken heart you needn't go to a doctor or minister with it; the best physician is the Great Physician.

TRUE WISDOM

In the book of Revelation we read: *"I heard a voice from heaven saying unto me, Write, Blessed are the dead which die in the Lord from henceforth: Yea, saith the Spirit, that they may rest from their labours; and their works do follow them."*

There are many mentioned in the Scriptures of whom we read that they lived so many years and then they died. The cradle and the grave are brought close together; they lived and they died, and that is all we know about them. So in these days you could write on the tombstone of a great many professing Christians that they were born on such a day and they died on such a day; there is nothing whatever between.

But there is one thing you cannot bury with a good man - his influence still lives. They have not buried Daniel yet; his influence is as great today as it ever was. Do you tell me that Joseph is dead? His influence still lives, and will continue to live on and on. You may bury the frail tenement of clay that a good man lives in, but you cannot get rid of his influence and example. Paul was never more powerful than he is today.

Do you tell me that John Howard, who went into so many of the dark prisons in Europe, is dead? Is Henry Martyn, or Wilberforce, or John Bunyan dead? Go into the Southern States, and there you will find thousands of men and women who once were slaves. Mention to any of them the name of Wilberforce, and see how quickly the eye will light up. He lived for something else beside himself, and his memory will never die out of the hearts of those for whom he lived and laboured.

Is Wesley or Whitefield dead? The names of those great evangelists were never more honoured than they are now. Is John Knox dead? You can go to any part of Scotland today, and feel the power of his influence.

I will tell you who are dead. The enemies of these servants of God - those who persecuted them and told lies about them. But the men themselves have outlived all the lies that were uttered concerning them. Not only that; they will shine in another world. How true are the words of the old Book: "They that be wise shall shine as the brightness of the firmament; and they that turn many to righteousness as the stars for ever and ever."

Let us go on turning as many as we can to righteousness. Let us be dead to the world, to its lies, its pleasures, and its ambitions. Let us live for God, continually going forth to win souls for Him.

THE STRENGTH OF THE ENEMY

The reason why so many Christians fail all through life is just this - they underestimate the strength of the enemy. My dear friend, you and I have got a terrible enemy to contend with. Do not let Satan deceive you. Unless you are spiritually dead, it means warfare. Nearly everything around tends to draw us away from God. We do not step clear out of Egypt on to the throne of God. There is the wilderness journey, and there are enemies in the land.

Do not let any man or woman think all he or she has to do is to join the Church. That will not save you. The question is, are you overcoming the world, or is the world overcoming you? Are you more patient than you were five years ago? Are you more amiable? If you are not, the world is overcoming you, even if you are a Church member. That epistle that Paul wrote to Titus says that we are to be sound in patience, faith, and charity. We have got Christians, a good many of them that are good in spots, but mighty poor generally. Just a little bit of them seems to be saved, you know. They are not rounded out in their characters. It is just because they have not been taught that they have a terrible foe to overcome.

If I wanted to find out whether a man was a Christian, I would not go to his minister. I would go and ask his wife. I tell you, we want more *home piety* just now. If a man does not treat his wife right, I do not want to hear him talk about Christianity. What is the use of his talking about salvation for the next life, if he has no salvation for this? We want a Christianity that goes into our homes and every-day lives. Some men's religion just repels me. They put on a whining voice and a sort of a religious tone, and talk so sanctimoniously on Sunday that you would think they were wonderful saints. But on Monday they are quite different. They put their religion away with their clothes, and you do not see any more of it until the next Sunday. You laugh; but let us look out that we do not belong to that class. My friend, we have got to have a higher type of Christianity, or the Church is gone. It is wrong for a man or woman to profess what they do not possess. If you are not overcoming temptations, the world is overcoming you. Just get on your knees and ask God to help you. Let us go to God and ask Him to search us. Let us ask Him to wake us up; and let us not think that just because we are Church members we are all right. We are all wrong if we are not getting victory over sin.

A LITTLE PERSECUTION

A great many men are overcome by a little *persecution*. Do you know, I do not think we have enough persecution nowadays. Some people say we have persecution that is just as hard to bear as in the Dark Ages. Anyway, I think it would be a good thing if we had a little of the old-fashioned kind just now. It would bring out the strongest characters, and make us all healthier. I have heard men get up in prayer meetings, and say they were going to make a few remarks, and then keep on till you would think they were going to talk all the week. If we had a little persecution, people of that kind would not talk so much. Spurgeon used to say some Christians would make good martyrs; they would burn well, they are so dry. If there were a few stakes for burning Christians, I think it would take all the piety out of some men. I admit they have not got much; but then if they are not willing to suffer a little persecution for Christ, they are not fit to be his disciples. We are told: "All that will live godly in Christ Jesus shall suffer persecution." Make up your mind to this: If the world has nothing to say against you, Jesus Christ will have nothing to say for you.

The most glorious triumphs of the Church have been won in times of persecution. The early Church was persecuted for about three hundred years after the crucifixion, but they were years of growth and progress. But then, as St. Augustine hath said, the cross passed from the scene of public executions to the diadem of the Caesars, and the downgrade movement began. When the Church has joined hands with the State, it has invariably retrograded in spirituality and effectiveness; but the opposition of the State has only served to purify it of all dross. It was persecution that gave Presbyterianism to Scotland. It was persecution that gave civil and religious freedom to this country.

How are we to overcome in time of persecution? Hear the words of Christ: "In the world ye shall have tribulation: but be of good cheer; I have overcome the world." Paul could testify that though persecuted, he was never forsaken; that the Lord stood by him and strengthened him, and delivered him out of all his persecutions and afflictions.

HUMILITY

There is no harder lesson to learn than the *lesson* of humility. It is not taught in the schools of men, only in the school of Christ. It is the rarest of all the gifts. Very rarely do we find a man or woman who is following closely the footsteps of the Master in meekness and in humility. I believe that it is the hardest lesson, which Jesus Christ had to teach his disciples while He was here upon earth. He said: "Learn of Me; for I am meek and lowly in heart" (Matthew 11: 29). It looked at first as though He had failed to teach it to the twelve men who had been with Him almost constantly for three years.

I believe that if we are humble enough we shall be sure to get a great blessing. After all, I think that more depends upon us than upon the Lord, because He is always ready to give a blessing and give it freely, but we are not always in a position to receive it. He always blesses the humble; and, if we can get down in the dust before Him, no one will go away disappointed. It was Mary at the feet of Jesus, who had chosen the "better part."

Did you ever notice the reason Christ gave for learning of Him? He might have said: "Learn of Me, because I am the most advanced thinker of the age. I have performed miracles that no man else has performed. I have shown my supernatural power in a thousand ways." But no: the reason He gave was that He was "meek and lowly in heart."

We read of the three men in Scripture whose faces shone, and all three were noted for their meekness and humility. We are told that the face of Christ shone at his transfiguration; Moses, after he had been in the mount for forty days, came down from his communion with God with a shining face; and when Stephen stood before the Sanhedrin on the day of his death, his face was lighted up with glory. If our faces are to shine we must get into the valley of humility, we must go down in the dust before God.

GET YOUR CHILDREN INTO THE ARK

I never speak to parents but I think of two fathers, one of whom lived on the banks of the Mississippi, the other in New York. The first one devoted all his time to amassing wealth. He had a son to whom he was much attached, and one day the boy was brought home badly injured. The father was informed that the boy could live but a short time, and he broke the news to his son as gently as possible. "You say I cannot live, father? Oh, then, pray for my soul," said the boy. In all those years that father had never said a prayer for that boy, and he told him he could not. Shortly after the boy died. That father has said since that he would give all that he possessed if he could call that boy back only to offer one short prayer for him.

The other father had a boy who had been sick some time, and he came home one day and found his wife weeping. She said: "I cannot help but believe that this is going to prove fatal."

The man started, and said: "If you think so, I wish you would tell him."

But the mother could not tell her boy. The father went to the sick room, and he saw that death was feeling for the cords of life, and he said: "My son, do you know you are not going to live? " The little fellow looked up and said: " No; is this death that I feel stealing over me? Will I die today?"

"Yes, my son, you cannot live the day out."

And the little fellow smiled and said: "Well, father, I shall be with Jesus tonight, shan't I?"

"Yes, you will spend the night with the Lord," and the father broke down and wept.

The little fellow saw the tears, and said: "Do not weep for me. I will go to Jesus and tell Him that ever since I can remember you have prayed for me."

I have three children, and if God should take them from me, I would rather have them take such a message home to Him than to have the wealth of the whole world. Oh, would to God I could say something to stir you, fathers and mothers, to get your children into the Ark.

FAITH

The keynote of all our work for God should be *faith*.

In all my life I have never seen men or women disappointed in receiving answers to their prayers, if those persons were full of faith, and had good grounds for their faith. Of course we must have a warrant in Scripture for what we expect. I am sure we have a good warrant in coming together to pray for a blessing on our friends and on this neighbourhood.

Unbelief is as much an enemy to the Christian as it is to the unconverted. It will keep back the blessing now as much as it did in the days of Christ. We read that in one place Christ could not do many mighty works, because of their unbelief. If Christ could not do this, how can we expect to accomplish anything if the people of God are unbelieving? I contend that God's children are alone able to hinder God's work. Infidels, atheists, and sceptics cannot do it. Where there is union, strong faith, and expectation among Christians, a mighty work is always done. In Hebrews we read that without faith it is impossible to please God. "For he that cometh to God must believe that He is, and that He is a Rewarder of them that diligently seek Him." That is addressed to us who are Christians, as much as to those who are seeking God for the first time. We are here today seeking a blessing on our friends. We want God to revive us, and also that the outlying masses may be reached. We read in this passage that God blesses those who "diligently seek Him." Let us diligently seek Him today; let us have great faith; and let our expectation be from God.

I remember when I was a boy, in the spring of the year, when the snow had melted away on the New England hills where I lived, I used to take a certain kind of glass and hold it up to the warm rays of the sun. These would strike on it, and I would set the woods on fire. Faith is the glass that brings the fire of God out of heaven. It was faith that drew the fire down on Carmel and burned up Elijah's offering. We have got the same God today, and the same faith. Some people seem to think that faith is getting old, and that the Bible is wearing out. But the Lord will revive His work now: and we shall be able to set the world on fire, if each believer has a strong and simple faith.

ENTHUSIASM

Eph. 5:14 *"Awake thou that sleepest, and arise from the dead, and Christ shall give thee light."*

I want to apply these words to the children of God. If the lost are to be reached by the Gospel of the Son of God, Christianity must be more aggressive than it has been in the past. We have been on the defensive long enough; the time has come for us to enter on a war of aggression. When we as children of God wake up and go to work in the vineyard, then those who are living in wickedness all about us will be reached; but not in any other way. You may go to mass meetings, and discuss the question of "How to reach the masses?" but when you have done with discussion you have to go back to personal effort. Every man and woman who loves the Lord Jesus Christ must wake up to the fact that he or she has a mission in the world, in this work of reaching the lost. A man may talk in his sleep; and it seems to me that there is a good deal of that kind of thing now in the Lord's work. A man may even preach in his sleep. A friend of mine sat up in his bed one night and preached a sermon right through. He was sound asleep all the time. Next morning his wife told him all about it. He preached the same sermon in his church the next Sabbath morning; I have got it in print; and a good sermon it is. So a man may not only talk, but also actually preach in his sleep.

There are many preachers in these days that are fast asleep.

There is one thing, however, that we must remember: a man cannot *work* in his sleep. There is no better way to wake up a church than to set it to work. One man will wake up another in waking himself up. Of course, the moment we begin a work of aggression, and declare war with the world, the flesh, and the devil, some wise head will begin to shake, and there will be the cry, "Zeal without knowledge!" I think I have heard that objection ever since I commenced the Christian life. I heard of someone who was speaking the other day of something that was to be done, and who said he hoped zeal would be tempered with moderation. Another friend very wisely replied, that he hoped moderation would be tempered with zeal. If that were always the case, Christianity would be like a red-hot ball rolling over the face of the earth. There is no power on earth that can stand before the onward march of God's people, when they are dead earnest.

CONFESSION

Another element in true prayer is *Confession*. I do not want Christian friends to think that I am talking to the unsaved. I think we, as Christians, have a good many sins to confess.

If you go back to the Scripture records, you will find that the men who lived nearest to God, and had most power with Him, were those who confessed their sins and failures. Daniel, as we have seen, confessed his sins and those of his people. Yet there is nothing recorded against Daniel. He was one of the best men then on the face of the earth; yet his confession of sin was one of the deepest and most humble on record. Brooks, referring to Daniel's Confession, says: "In these words you have seven circumstances that Daniel uses in confessing of his and the people's sins: and all to heighten and aggravate them. First, 'We have sinned'; secondly, 'We have committed iniquity'; thirdly, 'We have done wickedly'; fourthly, 'We have rebelled against Thee'; fifthly, 'We have departed from Thy precepts'; sixthly, 'We have not hearkened unto

Thy servants'; seventhly, 'Nor our princes, nor all the people of the land.' These seven aggravations which Daniel reckons up in his confession, are worthy our most serious consideration."

Job was no doubt a holy man, a mighty prince; yet he had to fall in the dust and confess his sins. So you will find it all through the Scriptures. When Isaiah saw the purity and holiness of God, he beheld himself in his true light; and he exclaimed, "Woe is me! for I am undone; because I am a man of unclean lips."

I firmly believe that the Church of God will have to confess their own sins, before there can be any great work of grace in London, or in any other place. There must be a deeper work among God's believing people. I sometimes think it is about time to give up preaching to the ungodly, and preach to those who profess to be Christians. If we had a higher standard of life in the Church of God, there would be thousands more flocking into the Kingdom. So it was in the past, when God's believing children turned away from their sins and their idols, then the fear of God fell upon the people round about. Take up the history of Israel, and you find that when they put away their strange gods, God visited the nation, and there came a mighty work of grace.

What we want in these days is a true and deep revival in the Church of God. I have little sympathy with the idea that God is going to reach the outlying masses by a cold and formal Church. The judgment of God must begin with us.

THANKSGIVING

It is said that in a time of great despondency among the first settlers in New England, it was proposed in one of their public assemblies to proclaim a fast. An old farmer arose; spoke of their provoking heaven with their complaints; reviewed their measures;

showed that they had much to be thankful for; and moved that instead of appointing a day of fasting, they should appoint a day of thanksgiving. This was done; and the custom has been continued ever since.

However great our difficulties, or deep even our sorrows, there is room for thankfulness. Thomas Adams has said, "Lay up in the ark of thy memory not only the pot of manna, the bread of life; but even Aaron's rod, the very scourge of correction, wherewith thou hast been bettered. Blessed be the Lord, not only giving, but also taking away, saith Job. The God that sees there is no walking upon roses to heaven, puts His children into the way of discipline; and by the fire of correction eats out the rust of corruption. God sends trouble, then bids us call upon Him; promiseth our deliverance; and lastly, all He requires of us is to glorify Him. 'Call upon Me in the day of trouble; I will deliver thee, and thou shalt glorify Me.' Like the nightingale, we can sing in the night, and say with John Newton,

" Since all that I meet shall work for my good,
The bitter is sweet, the medicine food;
Though painful at present, 'twill cease before long,
And then - oh, how pleasant - the conqueror's song."

Among all the apostles none suffered so much as Paul; but none of them do we find so often giving thanks as he. Take his letter to the Philippians. Remember what he suffered at Philippi; how they laid many stripes upon him, and cast him into prison. Yet every chapter in that Epistle speaks of rejoicing and giving thanks. There is that well known passage: "Be careful for nothing but in everything, by prayer and supplication, with thanksgiving, let your requests be made known unto God." As someone has said, there are here three precious ideas: "careful for nothing; prayerful for everything; and thankful for anything." We always get more by being thankful for what God has done for us.

UNITY

It is one of the most humiliating things in the present day to see how God's family is divided up. If we love the Lord Jesus Christ the burden of our hearts will be that God may bring us closer together, so that we may love one another and rise above all party feeling.

In repairing a church in one of the Boston wards the inscription upon the wall behind the pulpit was covered up. Upon the first Sabbath after repairs, a little five-year old whispered to her mother: "I know why God told the paint-men to cover that pretty verse up. It was because the people did not love one another." The inscription was: "A new commandment I give unto you, that ye love one another."

A Boston minister says he once preached on "The Recognition of Friends in the Future," and was told after the service by a hearer, that it would be more to the point to preach about the recognition of friends here, as he had been in the church twenty years and did not know any of its members.

I was in a little town in America some time ago. One night as I came out of the meeting, I saw another building where the people were coming out. I said to a friend, "Have you got two churches here?" "Oh yes," "How do you get on?" "Oh, we get on very well." "I am glad to hear that. Was your brother minister at the meeting?" "Oh no; we don't have anything to do with each other. We find that is the best way." And they called that "getting on very well." Oh, may God make us of one heart and of one mind! Let our hearts be like drops of water flowing together. Unity among the people of God is a sort of foretaste of heaven.

Did you ever notice that the last prayer Jesus Christ made on earth, before they led Him away to Calvary, was that His disciples might all be one? He could look down the stream of time, and see that divisions would come - how Satan would try to divide the flock of God. Nothing will silence infidels so quickly as Christians everywhere being united. Then our testimony will have weight with the ungodly and the careless. But when they see how Christians are divided, God will not work. The Holy Spirit is grieved, and there is little power where there is no unity,

If I thought I had one drop of sectarian blood in my veins, I would let it out before I went to bed; if I had one sectarian hair in my head, I would pull it out. Let us get right to the heart of Jesus Christ; then our prayers will be acceptable to God, and showers of blessings will descend.

FAITH AND FAILURE

1 John 5:4 *"Whatsoever is born of God overcometh the world: and this is the victory that overcometh the world, even our faith."*

Notice that everything human in this world fails. Every man the moment he takes his eye off God, has failed. Every man has been a failure at some period of his life. Abraham failed. Moses failed. Elijah failed. Take the men that have become so famous and that were so mighty - the moment they got their eye off God, they were weak like other men; and it is a very singular thing that those men failed on the strongest point in their character: I suppose it was because they were not on the watch. Abraham was noted for his faith, and he failed right there - he denied his wife. Moses was noted for his meekness and humility, and he failed right there - he got angry. God kept him out of the promised land because he lost his temper: I know he was called "the servant of God," and that he was a mighty man, and had power with God, but humanly speaking, he failed, and was kept out of the promised land. Elijah was noted for his power in prayer and for his courage, yet he became a coward. He was the boldest man of his day; and stood before Ahab, and the royal court, and all the prophets of Baal; yet when he heard that Jezebel had threatened his life, he ran away to the desert, and under a juniper tree prayed that he might die. Peter was noted for his boldness, and a little maid scared him nearly out of his wits. As soon as she spoke to him, he began to tremble, and he swore that he didn't know Christ. I have often said to myself that I'd like to have been there on the day of Pentecost alongside of that maid when she saw Peter preaching.

"Why," I suppose she said, "What has come over that man? He was afraid of *me* only a few weeks ago, and now he stands up before all Jerusalem and charges these very Jews with the murder of Jesus."

The moment he got his eye off the Master he failed; and every man, I don't care who he is - even the strongest - every man that hasn't Christ in him, is a failure. John, the beloved disciple, was noted for his meekness; and yet we hear of him wanting to call fire down from heaven on a little town because it had refused the common hospitalities.

A PLACE OF REFUGE

1 Peter 5:7 *"Casting all your care upon him; for he careth for you."*

A great many people seem to embalm their troubles. I always feel like running away when I see them coming. They bring out their old mummy; and tell you in a sad voice:

"You don't know the troubles I have!" My friends, if you go to the Lord with your troubles, He will take them away. Would you not rather be with the Lord and get rid of your troubles, than be with your troubles and without God? Let trouble come if it will drive us nearer to God.

It is a great thing to have a place of resort in the time of trouble. How people get on without the God of the Bible is a mystery to me. If I didn't have such a refuge, a place to go and pour out my heart to God in such times, I don't know what I would do. It seems as if I would go out of my mind. But to think, when the heart is burdened, we can go and pour it into His ear, and then have the answer come back, "I will be with him," there is comfort in that!

I thank God for the old Book. I thank God for this old promise. It is as sweet and fresh today as it has ever been. Thank God, none of those promises are out of date, or grown stale. They are as fresh and vigorous and young and sweet as ever.

WE CAN SAY WITH PAUL
Ps. 91:16 *"With long life will I satisfy him, and shew him my salvation."*

Jesus Christ came into the world to destroy death, and we can say with Paul, if we will, "Oh, death, where is thy sting?" And we can hear a voice rolling down from heaven saying, "Buried in the bosom of the Son of God." He took death unto His own bosom. He went into the grave to conquer and overthrow it, and when He arose from the dead said, "Because I live, ye shall live also." Thank God, we have a long life with Christ in glory.

My dear friends, if we are in Christ we are never going to die. Do you believe that? If sometime you should read that D. L. Moody, of East Northfield, is dead, don't believe a word of it. He has gone up higher, that is all; gone out of this old clay tenement into a house that is immortal, a body that death cannot touch, that sin cannot taint, a body fashioned like unto His own glorious body. Moses wouldn't have changed the body he had at the transfiguration for the body he had at Pisgah. Elijah wouldn't have changed the body he had at the transfiguration for the body he had under the juniper tree. They got better bodies; and I too am going to make something out of death.

TAKE YE AWAY THE STONE

In the gospel by John we read that at the tomb of Lazarus our Lord said to His disciples, "Take ye away the stone." Before the act of raising Lazarus could be performed, the disciples had their part to do. Christ could have removed the stone with a word. It would have been very easy for Him to have commanded it to roll away, and it would have obeyed His voice, as the dead Lazarus did when He called him back to life.

But the Lord would have His children learn this lesson: that they have something to do towards raising the spiritually dead. The disciples had not only to take away the stone, but after Christ had raised Lazarus they had to "loose and let him go."

It is a question if any man on the face of the earth has ever been converted. without God using some human instrument, in some way. God could easily convert men without us; but that is not His way.

The stone I want to speak about today, that must be rolled away before any great work of God can be brought about, is the miserable stone of prejudice.

Many people have a great prejudice against revivals; they hate the very word. I am sorry to say that this feeling is not confined to ungodly or careless people; there are not a few Christians who seem to cherish a strong dislike both to the word "Revival" and to the thing itself.

What does "Revival" mean? It simply means a recalling from obscurity - a finding some hidden treasure and bringing it back to the light. I think every one of us must acknowledge that we are living in a time of need. I doubt if there is a family in the world that has not some relative whom they would like to see brought into the fold of God, and who needs salvation.

Men are anxious for a revival in business. I am told that there is a widespread and general stagnation in business. People are very anxious that there should be revival of trade this winter. There is a great revival in politics just now. In all departments of life you find that men are very anxious for a revival in the things that concern them most.

If this is legitimate - and I do not say but it is perfectly right in its place - should not every child of God be praying for and desiring a revival of godliness in the world at the present time. Do we not need a revival of downright honesty, of truthfulness, of uprightness, and of temperance? Are there not many who have become alienated from the Church of God and from the house of the Lord, who are forming an attachment to the saloon? Are not our sons being drawn away by hundreds and thousands, so that while you often find the churches empty, the liquor shops are crowded every Sabbath afternoon and evening. I am sure the saloonkeepers are glad if they can have a revival in their business; they do not object to selling more whisky and beer. Then surely every true Christian ought to desire that men who are in danger of perishing eternally should be saved and rescued.

Some people seem to think that "Revivals" are a modern invention - that they have only been known within the last few years. But they are nothing new. If there is not Scriptural authority for revivals, then I cannot understand my Bible.

MOODY'S MOTTO

It is a great thing to lead one soul from the darkness of sin into the glorious light of the Gospel. I believe if an angel were to wing his way from earth up to heaven, and were to say that there was one poor, ragged boy, without father or mother - with no one to care for him and teach him the way of life; and if God were to ask who among them was willing to come down to this earth and live here for fifty years and lead that one to Jesus Christ, every angel in heaven would volunteer to go. Even Gabriel, who stands in the presence of the Almighty, would say: "Let me leave my high and lofty position, and let me have the luxury of leading one soul to Jesus Christ." There is no greater honour than to be the instrument in God's hand of leading one person out of the kingdom of Satan into the glorious light of heaven.

I have this motto in my Bible, and I commend it to you: "Do all the good you can; to all the people you can; in all the ways you can; and as long as ever you can." If each of us will at once set about some work for God, and will keep at it 365 days in the year, then a good deal will be accomplished. Let us so live that it may be truthfully said of us: We have done what we could.

THE EIGHTH CHAPTER OF ROMANS

The eighth chapter of Romans is one of the most famous chapters in all of Paul's epistles. I say, one of the most famous. There are three chapters that I think are high-water mark, and when I get into one of them I think that is the best, and when I get into the second one, I think that is the best, and when I get into the third, I think that is the best. I have three children; I think they are all the best. I can't tell which I like the best, but I like all three of them.

The 13th chapter of I Corinthians, that treatise on love, is sublime, and if the church of God could live in that chapter for twelve months, I believe it would revolutionize this country. I am quite sure the church of God itself would be revolutionized. Or the 15th chapter of I Corinthians, where Paul tells us what the gospel is, how Christ died for our sins and how He was raised for our justification, and where he teaches the mighty doctrine of the resurrection and the precious truth of His coming again; when I get there, I think that is about the best chapter. And then I turn to the 8th chapter of Romans, and when I get right into the heart of it, I really think that it is the best chapter Paul ever wrote.

This is the chapter that opens with no condemnation and closes with no separation. But mark you, it doesn't say there are no faults, no infirmities; it says there is no condemnation, either in life, or in death, or at the judgment. A great many people live all their lifetime under the bondage of death, and they fear the judgment; but if a man's life is hid with Christ in God, there is nothing to fear in time or in eternity. There is nothing that will give the believer so much comfort as to know his standing in Christ.

Note that the difference between a believer and an unbeliever is right here. An unbeliever is living in his day, and he has nothing but a long dark eternal night to look forward to; a Christian is now living his night, and he has a grand morning that he is looking forward to. The day is ahead, the glory is ahead, the best of life is ahead; it is not behind. That is the teaching of Scripture; and for a man whose life is hid with Christ in God, judgment is already passed; he will not come into judgment. Christ was judged for me, and the judgment is behind me, instead of before me. John 5:24: "Verily, verily, I say unto you, He that heareth my word, and believeth on him that sent me, hath everlasting life, and shall not come into condemnation; but is passed from death unto life." Already passed from death unto life.

THE FOURTH COMMANDMENT

Exodus 20:8-11 *"Remember the sabbath day, to keep it holy. Six days shalt thou labour, and do all thy work: but the seventh day is the sabbath of the Lord thy God: in it thou shalt not do any work, thou, nor thy son, nor thy daughter, thy manservant, nor thy maidservant, nor thy cattle, nor thy stranger that is within thy gates: for in six days the Lord made heaven and earth, the sea, and all that in them is, and rested the seventh day: wherefore the Lord blessed the sabbath day, and hallowed it."*

There has been an awful letting-down in this country regarding the Sabbath, and many a man has been shorn of spiritual power, like Samson, because he is not straight on this question. Can *you* say that you observe the Sabbath properly? You may be a professed Christian: are you obeying this commandment? Or do you neglect the house of God on the Sabbath day, and spend your time drinking and carousing in places of vice and crime, showing contempt for God and His law? Are you ready to step onto the scales? Where were you last Sabbath? How did you spend it?

I honestly believe that this commandment is just as binding today as it ever was. I have talked with men who have said that it has been abrogated, but they have never been able to point to any place in the Bible where God repealed it. When Christ was on earth, He did nothing to set it aside. He freed it from the traces under which the scribes and Pharisees had put it, and gave it its true place. "The Sabbath was made for man, not man for the Sabbath." It is just as practicable and as necessary for men today as it ever was - in fact, more than ever, because we live in such an intense age.

The Sabbath was binding in Eden, and it has been in force ever since. The fourth commandment begins with the word "remember," showing that the Sabbath already existed when God wrote this law on the tables of stone at Sinai. How can men claim that this one commandment has been done away with when they will admit that the other nine are still binding?

I believe that the Sabbath question today is a vital one for the whole country. It is the burning question of the present time. If you give up the Sabbath the church goes; if you give up the church the home goes; and if the home goes the nation goes. That is the direction in which we are travelling.

The church of God is losing its power on account of so many people's giving up the Sabbath, and using it to promote selfishness.

"Sabbath" means "rest," and the meaning of the word gives a hint as to the true way to observe the day. God rested after creation, and ordained the Sabbath as a rest for man. He blessed it and hallowed it. "Remember the rest-day to keep it holy." It is the day when the body may be refreshed and strengthened after six days of labour, and the soul drawn into closer fellowship with its Maker.

THE PRECIOUS BLOOD.

In I Peter 1:18,19 we read: *"Forasmuch as ye know that ye were not redeemed with corruptible things, as silver and gold, from your vain conversation received by tradition from your fathers; But with the precious blood of Christ, as of a lamb without blemish and without spot."*

Peter was an old man when he wrote those words. I suppose the blood of Jesus grew more precious to him as the years went by.

Now why is it precious? It is precious because *it redeems us.* Not only from the hands of the devil, but from the hands of the law. It redeems me from the curse of the law; it brings me out from under the law. The law condemns me, but Christ has satisfied the claims of the law. He tasted death for every man, and He has made it possible for every man to be saved. Paul says, God gave Him up freely for us all, and what we want to do is to take Him.

Silver and gold could not redeem our souls.

Our life had been forfeited. Death had come into the world by sin, and nothing but blood could atone for the soul. If gold and silver could have redeemed us, do you not think that God would have created millions of worlds full of gold? It would have been an easy matter for Him. But we are not redeemed by such corruptible things, but by the precious blood of Christ. Redemption means "buying back"; we had sold ourselves for naught, and Christ redeemed us and bought us back. A friend in Ireland once met a little Irish boy who had caught a sparrow. The poor little bird was trembling in his hand, and seemed very anxious to escape. The gentleman begged the boy to let it go, as the bird could not do him any good; but the boy said he would not, for he had chased it three hours before he could catch it. He tried to reason it out with the boy, but it vain. At last he offered to buy the bird. The boy agreed to the price, and it was paid. Then the gentleman took the poor little thing, and held it out on his hand. The boy had been holding it very fast, for the boy was stronger than the bird, just as Satan is stronger than we; and there it sat for a time scarcely able to realize the fact that it had got liberty; but in a little while it flew away chirping, as if to say to the gentleman: "Thank you! Thank you! You have redeemed me." That is what redemption is - buying back and setting free. Christ came to break the fetters of sin, to open the prison doors and set the sinner free.

5

THE BEST OF MOODY'S SERMONS

❦

THE NEW BIRTH
John 3:3: *"Jesus answered and said unto him, Verily, verily, I say unto thee, Except a man be born again, he cannot see the kingdom of God."*

SUPPOSE I PUT THE QUESTION TO THIS AUDIENCE, AND ASK HOW MANY BELIEVE IN THE WORD OF GOD, I HAVE no doubt every man and every woman would rise and say, "I believe." There might be an infidel or sceptic here and there, but undoubtedly the great mass would say they believed. Then what are you going to do with this solemn truth, "Except a man be born again, he cannot see the kingdom of God," much less inherit it? There are a great many mysteries in the Word of God. There are a great many dark sayings of which we have not yet discovered the depth. But God has put that issue so plainly and simply that he who runs may read if he will. This third chapter of St. John makes the way to Heaven plainer than any other chapter in the Bible; yet there is no truth so much misunderstood, and the church and the world are so troubled about, as this. Let me just say, before I go any further, what regeneration is not. It is not going to church. How many men think they are converted because they go to church! I come in contact with many men who say they are Christians because they go to church regularly. It is a wrong idea that the devil never frequents any place but billiard-halls, saloons, and theatres; wherever the Word of God is preached, he is there. He is in this audience today. You may go to church all the days of your life, and yet not be converted. Going to church is not being born again. But there is another class who say, "I don't place my hopes in going to church. I have been baptized, and I think I was regenerated when that took place." Where do those persons get their evidence? Certainly not in the Bible. You cannot baptize men into regeneration. If you could, I would go up and down the world and baptize every man, woman, and child; and if I could not do it when they were awake, I would do it while they slept. But the Word says, "Except a man be born again" - born in the Spirit, born in righteousness from above - "he cannot see the kingdom of God."

There is another class who say, " I was born again when I was confirmed. I was confirmed when I was five years old." But confirmation is not regeneration. A new birth must be the work of God, and not the work of man. Baptism, confirmation, and other ordinances are right in their place, but the moment you build hope on them instead of on new birth, you are being deceived by Satan. Another man says, "That is not what my hope is based upon; I say my prayers regularly." I suppose there was no man prayed more regularly than Paul did before Christ met him; he was a praying man. But saying prayers is one thing, and praying is another. Saying prayers is not conversion. You may pray from education; your mother may have taught you when you were a little boy. I remember that I could not go to sleep when I was a little boy unless I said my prayers, and yet perhaps the very next word I uttered might be an oath. There is just as much virtue in counting beads as in saying prayers, unless the heart has been regenerated and born again.

There is another class who say, "I read the Bible regularly." Well, reading the Bible is very good, and prayer is very good in its place; but you don't see anything in the Scriptures which says, "Except a man read the Bible he cannot see the kingdom of God." There is still another class who say, "I am trying to do the best I can, and I will come out all right." That is not new birth at all; that is not being born of God. Trying to do the best you can is not regeneration. This question of new birth is the most important that ever came before the world, and it ought to be settled in every man's mind. Everyone should inquire, Have I been born of the Spirit? Have I passed from death unto life? Or am I building my hopes of Heaven on some form? In the first chapter of Genesis we find God working alone; He went on creating the world all alone. Then we find Christ coming to Calvary alone. His disciples forsook Him, and in redemption He was alone. And when we get to the third chapter of John we find that the work of regeneration is the work of God alone. The Ethiopian cannot change his skin, nor the leopard his spots; we are born in sin, and the change of heart must come from God. We believe in the good old Gospel.

What man wants is to come to God for this new heart. The moment he gets it he will work for the Lord. He cannot help it; it becomes his second nature. Some say, "I would like to have you explain this new birth." Well, I might as well be honest, and own right up that I cannot explain it. I have read a great many books and sermons trying to explain the philosophy of it, but they all fail to do it. I don't understand how it is done. I cannot understand how God created the earth. It staggers me and bewilders me when I think how God created nature out of nothing. But, say the infidels, He did not do it. Then how did He do it? A man came to me in Scotland, and said he could explain it, and I asked him how those rocks are made. He said, "They are made from sand." "What makes the sand?" "Oh" he replied, "Rocks." "Then," I asked him, "what made the first sand?" He couldn't tell. Notwithstanding the philosophy of some people, we do believe that God did create the world. We believe in redemption. We believe that Christ came from the Father, and that He grew up and taught men. We believe He went into the sepulchre and burst the bands of death. You may ask me to explain all this; but I don't know how to do it. You ask me to explain regeneration. I cannot do it. But one thing I know - that I have been regenerated. All the infidels and sceptics could not make me believe differently. I feel a different man than I did twenty-one years ago last March, when God gave me a new heart. I have not sworn since that night, and I have no desire to swear. I delight to labour for God, and all the influences of the world cannot convince me that I am not a different man. I heard some time ago about four or five commercial travellers going to hear a minister preach. When they got back to their hotel, they began to discuss the sermon. A good many people just go to church for the purpose of discussing those things, but they should remember that they must be spiritually inclined to understand spiritual things. Those travellers came to the wise conclusion that the minister did not know what he was talking about. An old man heard them say they would not believe anything unless they could reason it out, and he went up to them and said: "While I was coming down in the train this morning I noticed in a field some sheep, some geese, some swine, and cattle eating grass. Can you tell me by what process that grass is turned into hair, feathers, wool, and horns?" "No," they answered, "not exactly." "Well, do you believe it is done?" "Oh, yes, we believe that." "But," said the old man, "you said you could not believe anything unless you understood it." "Oh," they answered, "we cannot help believing that; we see it." Well, I cannot help believing that I am regenerated, because I feel it. Christ explained it to Nicodemus thus, "The wind bloweth where it listeth, and thou hearest the sound thereof, but canst not tell whence it cometh, and whither it goeth." Can you tell all about the currents of the air? He says it is everyone that is born of the Spirit. Suppose, because I never saw the wind, I say it was all false. I have lived nearly forty years, and I never saw the wind. I never saw a man that ever did see it. I can imagine that little girl down there saying, "That man doesn't know as much as I do. Didn't the wind blow my hat off the other day? Haven't I felt the effects of the wind? Haven't I felt it beating against my face?" And I say you never saw the effects of the wind any more than a child of God felt the Spirit working in his heart. He knows that his eyes have been opened; that he has been born of the Spirit; that he has got another nature, a heart that goes up to God, after he has been born of the Spirit. It seems to me this is perfectly reasonable.

We have a law that no man shall be elected President unless he was born on American soil. I never heard anyone complain of that law. We have Germans, Scandinavians, foreigners coming here from all parts of the world, and I never heard a man complain of that law. Haven't we got a right to say who shall reign? Had I any right when I was in England, where a Queen reigns, to interfere? Has a foreigner any right to interfere here? Has not the God of Heaven a right to say how a man shall come into His kingdom, and who shall come? And He says: "Except a man be born again, he cannot see the kingdom." How are you going to get in? Going to try to educate men? That is what men are trying to do, but it is not God's way. A man is not much better after he is educated if he hasn't got God in his heart. Other men say, "I will work my way up." That is not God's way, and the only way is God's way - to be born again. Heaven is a prepared place for a prepared people. You take an unregenerated man in Chicago and put him on the crystal pavements of Heaven, and it would be hell. A man that can't bear to spend one Sunday among God's people on earth, with all their imperfections, what is he going to do among those who have made their robes white in the blood of the Lamb? He would say that was hell for him. Take the unregenerated man and put him into the very shadow of the Tree of Life, and he wouldn't want to sit there. A man who is born of the Spirit becomes a citizen of another world. He has been translated into new life, taken out of the power of darkness, and translated into the Kingdom of Light. Haven't you seen all around you men who had become suddenly and entirely changed?

Just draw a picture: Suppose we go down into one of these alleys - and I have been into some pretty dark holes down here in this alley that used to lie back of Madison street, and I have seen some pretty wretched homes. Go to one of those rooms, and you find a wife, with her four or five children. The woman is heart-broken. She is discouraged. When she married that man he swore to protect, love, and care for her, and provide for all her wants. He made good promises and kept them, for a few years, and did love her. But he got led away into one of these drinking saloons. He was a noble-hearted man by nature, and those are just the ones that are led astray. He has now become a confirmed drunkard. His children can tell by his footfall that he comes home drunk. They look upon him as a monster. The wife has many a scar on her body that she has received from that man's arm who swore to love and protect her. Instead of being a kind-hearted husband, he has become a demon. He doesn't provide for that poor woman. What a struggle there is. And may God have mercy upon the poor drunkard and his family is my prayer constantly. Suppose he is here in that gallery up there, or in the dark back there, and you can't see him. Maybe he is so ashamed of himself that he has got behind, a post. He hears that he may be regenerated; that God will take away the love of strong drink, and snap the fetters that have been binding him, and make him a free man, and he says, "By the grace of God I will ask Him to give me a new heart." And he says, "O God, save me!" Then he goes home. His wife says, "I never saw my husband look so happy for years. What has come over him?" He says, "I have been up there to hear these strangers. I heard Mr. Sankey singing 'Jesus of Nazareth passeth by,' and it touched my heart. The sermon about being born again touched my heart, and, wife, I just prayed right there, and asked God to give me a new heart, and I believe He has done it. Come, wife, pray with me!" And there they kneel down and erect the family altar.

Three months hence you go to that home, and what do you find? All is changed. He is singing "Rock of Ages, cleft for me," or that other hymn his mother once taught him, "There is a fountain filled with blood." His children have their arms upon his neck. That is Heaven upon earth. The Lord God dwells there. That man is passed from death unto life. That is the conversion we are aiming at. The man is made better, and that is what God does when a man has the spirit of Heaven upon him. He regenerates them, re-creates them in His own image. Let us pray that every man here who has the love of strong drink may be converted. Unite in prayer with me now and ask God to save these men that are rushing on to death and ruin.

WEIGHED IN THE BALANCE
Daniel 5:27: *'TEKEL; Thou art weighed in the balances, and art found wanting.'*

YOU WILL FIND MY TEXT TONIGHT IN ONE SHORT WORD, "TEKEL," MEANING: "THOU ART WEIGHED IN THE balances and art found wanting." In the fifth chapter of Daniel we read the history of the King Belshazzar. It is very short. Only one chapter tells us all we know about him. One short night of his career is all we see. He just seems to burst upon the stage and then disappears. We are told that he gave a great feast, and at this feast he had 1,000 of his lords, and they were drinking and praising the gods of silver, of gold, of brass, of iron, and of wood, out of the vessels which had been brought from the temple at Jerusalem. As they were drinking out of these vessels of gold from the house of God - I don't know but what it was at the midnight hour, all at once came forth the fingers of a man's hand and began to write upon the wall of the hall.

The king turns deathly pale, his knees shake together, and he trembles from head to foot. Perhaps if someone had told him the time was coming when he would be put into the balance and weighed he would have laughed at him. But he knows the vital hour has come, and that hand has written his doom in the words "MENE, MENE, TEKEL, UPHARSIN." He calls the wise men of his kingdom, and the man who can interpret this will be made the third ruler of his kingdom, and be clothed in scarlet, and have a chain about his neck. One after another tried, but no uncircumcised eye could make it out. He was greatly troubled. At last one was spoken of who had been able to interpret the dream of his father Nebuchadnezzar. He was told if he would send for Daniel he might interpret the writing. And now the prophet came in and looked upon the handwriting, and told him how his father had gone against God, and how he, Belshazzar, had gone against the Lord of Heaven, and how his reign was finished. And this was the writing: "MENE: God hath numbered thy kingdom, and finished it; TEKEL: Thou art weighed in the balances, and art found wanting; PERES: Thy kingdom is divided, and given to the Medes and Persians. The trial is over, the verdict is rendered, and the sentence brought out. That very night the king was hurled from his throne. That very night the army of Darius came tearing down the streets, and you might have heard the clash of arms, shouts of war, and have seen the king's blood mingling with the wine in that banquet hall.

Now I want to call your attention to that word "TEKEL." We are weighed in the balance. Now you cavil at the word of God; you make light when all is going well in the hour of your prosperity. But when the time of trial comes, and we are called into judgment, it will be altogether different. Suppose the sentence should come down from heaven upon every man and woman in this tabernacle to be weighed in the balance tonight, how would it be with you? Come, my friends, are you ready to be weighed tonight? Not in our own scales, but in God's balance. Suppose the scales were dropped now from the kingdom of God; are you ready to step into the balance and be weighed? Are you willing to be weighed by the law? I can imagine some of you saying, "I wouldn't be weighed by that law (meaning the decalogue); I don't believe it." Some men think we are away beyond the Mosaic law; we have got out of it. Why, Christ said in the fifth chapter of Matthew: "Think not that I am come to destroy the law, or the prophets; I am not come to destroy, but to fulfil. Heaven and earth may pass away, but my law shall never pass away"; but not until heaven and earth shall be removed will the word of God be removed. Now the commandments that I read to you tonight are as binding as ever they have been. Many men say that we have no need of the commandments, only the sermon on the Mount. "Think not that I am come to destroy the law, or the prophets: I am not come to destroy, but to fulfil." Now, my friends, are you ready to be weighed by the law of the God - by that magic law? What is the first commandment? "Thou shalt have no other gods before me." Are you ready to be weighed by this commandment? Now, the question is, have you fulfilled, or are you ready to fulfil, all the requirements of this law? A great many people say if they keep the commandments they don't need Christ. But have you kept them? I will admit if you keep the commandments you can be saved by them, but is there a man in this audience who can truly say that he has done this? Young lady, can you say: "I am ready to be weighed by the law tonight?" Can you, young man? Now, suppose we have these commandments written upon pieces of iron. You know when you go into a grocery store you see them taking a weight and putting it into the scales against what you have bought. Now, suppose the pieces of iron as weights and the law of *God* written on them. Take this first commandment, "Thou shalt have no other gods before me" upon one of the weights. Put it in one of the scales and just step on the other. "Thou art weighed in the balance." Is your heart set upon *God* tonight? Have you no other idol? Do you love Him above father or mother, the wife of your bosom, your children, home or land, wealth or pleasure? Have you got another god before Him? If you have, surely you are not ready against that commandment, "Thou shalt have no other god before me." That is the commandment of *God,* and it is binding tonight. Then take another. You will say there is no trouble about this one. We might go off to other ages or other lands, and we can find people who worship idols, but we have none here. But how many idols have we in our hearts? Many a man says, "Give me money and I will give you heaven; what care I for all the glories and treasures of heaven; give me treasures here. I don't care for heaven. I want to be a successful businessman." They make money and business their god. Although they don't make gods of silver and gold, they bow before them. There are more men who worship silver and gold in Chicago than any other god. But take another one: "Thou shalt not take the name of the Lord thy *God* in vain." Is there a swearing man ready to put the weight into the scales and step in? Young man, have you been taking the name of the Lord in vain today? What does he say? "The Lord will not hold him guiltless that taketh His name in vain." I don't believe men would ever have been guilty of swearing unless *God* had told them not to. They don't swear by their friends, by their fathers and mothers, by their wives, by their children. But because *God* has forbidden it, man wants to show how he despises. His law. "Thou shalt not take the name of the Lord thy *God* in vain." Blasphemer, go into the scales, and see how quick you will fly out. You will be like a feather in the balance. A great many men think there is nothing very serious in swearing; they don't think there's much wrong in it. Bear in mind that He sees something in it when He says: "Thou shalt not take the name of the Lord thy God in vain." You cannot trifle with God. Some men say they never swear except when they get angry. Suppose you swear only once in six months, or a year - suppose you swear once in ten years, do you, think God will hold you guiltless for that one act? A man that swears once shows that his heart is rebellious to God. What are you going to do, blasphemer? If the balances were here tonight, and God told you to step in, what would you do?

But take the fourth commandment: "Remember the Sabbath day to keep it holy." Suppose you could see the law written over those walls, "Remember the Sabbath day to keep it holy," could you say that you had observed it? Are you ready to be weighed by the weight, "Remember the Sabbath day to keep it holy"? Some of us may be professed Christians, but do we observe the Sabbath? If this country falls into neglect of the observance of the Sabbath, it will go the way of France, Mexico and Spain. Every nation that gives up the Sabbath must go down. It is only a question of time with them. Look when the children of Israel refused to obey the injunctions of the Lord in regard to the cultivation of their land, how He took them into bondage and kept them for seventy years to let them know that God's land was not to be trampled under their feet. Are you guilty or not guilty or innocent in regard to this law: "Thou shalt keep the Sabbath day holy"?

When I was in France in 1867, I could not tell one day from another. On Sunday stores were open, buildings were being erected, the same as on other days. See how quick that country went down. Only a few years ago it stood breast to breast with other nations, it stood side by side almost with England. But it didn't have any respect for the Sabbath: it trampled God's message under foot, and when the hour of battle came, God left them alone. My friends, every nation that tramples the Sabbath under its feet must go to ruin. Are you innocent or guilty? Do you keep the Sabbath day holy or not? I have been talking to those car conductors - and if there's any class of men I pity more than another it is them - and they have to work on the Sabbath. Some of you are breaking this law by coming down here on Sunday in the cars. What will you do? Foot it. It will be better for you. I make a point of never allowing myself to break the Sabbath of any man. When I was in London, and it's a pretty big city, you know, in my ignorance I made arrangements to preach four times at different places one Sunday. After I had made the appointments I found I had to walk sixteen miles, and I walked it, and I slept that night with a clear conscience. I want no hack-man to rise up in judgment against me. My friends, if we want to help the Sabbath, let business men and Christians never patronize cars on the Sabbath. I would hate to own stock in those horse-car companies, to be the means of taking the Sabbath from these men, and have to answer for it at the day of judgment. No man can work seven days a week and save his soul. And the very best thing we have is being taken from these men by us Christians. Are you willing to step into the balance and be weighed against "Thou shalt keep the Sabbath day holy"?

Well, there is the fifth: "Honour thy father and thy mother." Are you ready to be weighed against this? Have you honoured them? Is there anyone here tonight who is dishonouring father or mother? Now, I've lived nearly forty years, and I've learned one thing if I've learned nothing else, that no man or woman who treats disrespectfully father or mother ever prospers. How many young ladies have married against their father's wishes, and gone off and just made their own ruin. I never knew one case that did not turn out bad. They brought ruin upon themselves. This is a commandment from heaven: "Honour thy father and thy mother." In the last days men shall be disobedient to parents, void of natural affection; and it seems as if we were living in those days now. How many sons treat their mothers with contempt, make light of their entreaties. God says, "Honour thy father and thy mother." If the balances were placed in this hall would you be ready to step into them against this commandment? You may make light of it and laugh at it, but young men, remember that God will hedge your way. No man shall succeed that disobeys His commandment. But bear in mind you are not going to be weighed only against this solitary commandment - every weight will be put in.

"Thou shalt not kill." Most of you say, "That doesn't touch me at all; I never killed anyone; I'm no murderer." Look at that sermon on the Mount, which men think so much of. Look at it. Did you never in your heart wish a man dead who had done you an injury? That's murder. How are you? Innocent or guilty? If you have, you are a murderer at heart. Now, come, my friends, are you ready to be weighed against the law? Ah, if most of us were weighed tonight we would find this word written against us: "TEKEL," thou art weighed in the balance and found wanting.

But, let us take another, "Thou shalt not commit adultery." I don't know any sin that afflicts us like this. It is a very delicate subject to approach, but I never preach without being compelled to touch upon it. Young men among us are being bound hand and foot with this evil. Young men, hear this law tonight: "Thou shalt not commit adultery." Are you guilty even in thought? How many would come into the Tabernacle but that they are tied hand and foot, as one has been in the halls of vice, and some harlot, whose feet are fastened in hell, clings to him and says: "If you give me up, I will expose you." Can you step on the scales and take that harlot with you? "Thou shalt not commit adultery." You may think that no one knows your doings; you may think that they are all concealed; but God knows it. He that covers his sins shall not prosper. Out with it tonight. Confess it to your God. Ask Him to snap the fetters that bind you to this sin; ask Him to give you victory over your passions, and shake yourself like Samson and say, "By the grace of God I will not go down to hell with a harlot," and God will give you power. "Thou shalt not commit adultery." As I said the other night, I don't know a quicker way to hell. How many men have by their lecherous life broken their mothers' heart and gone down to their grave rotten, leaving the effect of their sin to their posterity?

Well, let us take up the next. "Thou shalt not steal." How many have been stealing today! I may be speaking to some clerk, who perhaps today took five cents out of his employer's drawer to buy a cigar, perhaps he took ten cents to get a shave, and thinks he will put it back tomorrow; no one will ever know it. If you have taken a penny you are a thief. Do you ever think how those little stealings may bring you to ruin? Let an employer find it out. If he don't take you into the courts, he will discharge you. Your hopes will be blasted, and it will be hard work to get up again. Whatever condition you are in, do not take a cent that does not belong to you. Rather than steal go up to heaven in poverty - go up to heaven from the poor house - and be honest rather than go through the world in a gilded chariot of stolen riches. A man who takes money that does not belong to him never gets any comfort. He never has any pleasure, for he has a guilty conscience. "Thou shalt not steal." Are you ready to be weighed tonight in the balances?

Then let us take the ninth commandment: "Thou shalt not bear false witness against thy neighbour," or, in other words, thou shalt not be guilty of lying. If you had a chance to make $200 or $300 are you not willing to go into a court and lie to get it? "Thou shalt not bear false witness against thy neighbour." Are you ready to step into the balances against this? Then take another. "Thou shalt not covet thy neighbour's goods." Are you innocent or guilty? How many times I used to covet that which belonged to other people before I was converted. I believe that is one of the greatest sins among us. My friends, how is it? Innocent or guilty? But suppose you are innocent of all these ten commandments, let us take that eleventh commandment of Christ's: "A new commandment I give unto you; thou shalt love one another." My friends, how is it tonight? Is love reigning in your hearts? Do you love your neighbours? Do you try to do them good, or are you living a life of selfishness, merely for yourself.

Now I can imagine that nearly every man or woman is saying to himself or herself, "If we are to be judged by these laws how are we going to be saved?" Every one of them has been broken by all people. The moral man is just as guilty as the rest. There is not a moralist in Chicago who, if he steps into those scales, can be saved; "except a man be born again, he cannot see the kingdom of God." "Except ye repent ye shall all perish." That is on one side of the scales, and he will see on the other, "Except ye be converted ye shall not enter the kingdom of God." I have heard a good many Pharisees saying, "These meetings are reaching the drunkards and gamblers and harlots; they are doing good"; but they don't think they need these meetings. They are all right; they are moral men. "Except a man be born again, he cannot see the kingdom of God." I don't care how moral he is. Nicodemus was probably one of the most moral men of his day. He was a teacher of the law; yet Christ said: "Except a man be born again, he cannot see the kingdom of God." I would a good deal rather preach to thieves and drunkards and vagabonds, than preach to self-righteous Pharisees. You don't have to preach to those men weeks and months to convince them that they are sinners. When a man learns that he has need of God, and that he is a sinner, it is very easy to reach him. But, my friends, the self-righteous Pharisee needs salvation as much as any drunkard that walks the streets of Chicago. There is another class I want to speak of. If I had time I would just like to take up the different classes in the city. That class is the rum-sellers. Put the rum-sellers in the balances. They ignore God's laws, but by and by He will say to them, "TEKEL," "Woe be to the man that put the bottle to his neighbour's lips." My friends, I would rather have that right hand cut off before I would give the bottle to a man. I would rather have my right arm cut off than deal out death and damnation to my fellow-men. If any poor drunkard here should be summoned into eternity tonight - weighed in the balances, what would he hear? "No drunkard shall inherit the kingdom of God." I can see how he would reel and stagger when he heard that. "No drunkard shall inherit the kingdom of heaven."

My friends, if you don't repent of your sins and ask Him for mercy, there is no hope for you. Let me ask you tonight to take this question home to yourself. If a summons should come at midnight to be weighed in the balances, what will become of your souls, because the law of God must be kept. Now there are many of you only making professions. You belong to the First Methodist Church, or you may be a member of a Baptist Church, but are you ready to be weighed - ready to step into these scales tonight? I think a great many would be found like those five foolish virgins. When the hour came they would be found with no oil in their lamps. If there is a person here tonight who has only an empty lamp, or is living on mere formalism, I beg of you to give it up. Give up that dead, cold, miserable luke warmness. God will spit it out of His mouth. He will have none of it. Wake up. Some of you have gone almost to sleep while I have been trying to weigh you in the balances. God will weigh you, and then if you have not Christ it will be "TEKEL."

I can imagine some of you saying: "I would just like Moody to put those tests to himself. I wonder what would become of him." My dear friends, if God was to ask me tonight I would tell Him "I am ready." I don't say this in any spirit of egotism, of self-righteousness, remember. If you ask me if I have broken the law of Moses, I would answer "Yes, sir." Ask me if I have broken the commandments: "Yes, sir." You may ask me then how I am ready to be weighed. If I step into the scales tonight the Son of God will step into the scales with me. I would not dare to go into them without Him. If I did, how quick the scales would go up. If a man has not got Christ, when the hour comes for him to be weighed, it will be "TEKEL, TEKEL, TEKEL." How are you tonight, my friend - ready to be weighed? (pointing to one of the audience) .

Answer - Yes, sir.

Mr. Moody - Have you got Christ?

Answer - Yes, sir.

Mr. Moody - That's right. Suppose I put the question to every man and woman in this audience. How quick many of them would begin to colour up. Oh, my friends, if you haven't got Him, get Him tonight. May God open your eyes and your minds to receive Him before you leave this Tabernacle tonight. Christ kept the law; Christ was the end of the law. If He had broken the law He would have had to die for Himself; but He kept it, and we are enabled to be clothed in righteousness. My friends, it is the height of madness to go out of this hall tonight and run the risk of being called by God and have to answer without Him. Now is the day and hour to accept salvation, and then He will be with us. Then there will be no alarm with us. I pity those Christian people who are afraid of death. They need not be afraid of death if they have Him. When He is with us it is only a translation. We are absent from the body to be present with the Lord. Here is the gospel of Jesus Christ. Will you be saved tonight? If you do not, when by and by God summons you into these scales, it will be written over you: "TEKEL, TEKEL; thou art weighed in the balances and art found wanting." My friends, what will you do tonight? Remain as you are and be lost, or accept salvation and be saved? Let us pray.

EXCUSES
Luke 14:18: *"And they all with one consent began to make excuse. The first said unto him. I have bought a piece of ground, and I must needs go and see it: I pray thee have me excused."*

THOSE MEN THAT HAD BEEN INVITED TO THIS FEAST WANTED TO BE EXCUSED. BEAR IN MIND THAT IT WAS to a feast that they were invited - not to a funeral - not to hear some dry, stupid sermon, nor to hear some dry lecture; they were not invited to go to prison, nor were they invited to go to a madhouse, but they were invited to go to a supper. And in all my travels I never met a man yet that really didn't like to go to a feast, especially if it was a royal feast. It is not very often that common people like us get an invitation to go to a royal feast; but I have got one here tonight. There isn't a man hardly in all of London but would consider it a great honour if he should get an invitation from Her Majesty to go to Windsor Castle to a feast she was giving in honour of her son that has returned from Russia with his young bride. Why, you know, if the honourable men in London get an invitation they would like it to get into the press and to have it noised abroad that they had been invited. They consider it a great honour; but there is something worth a great deal more than that tonight. Here is an invitation from the King of kings and the Lord of lords.

We read that down in the evening of this dispensation the marriage supper of the Lamb is to take place, and now God is sending out the invitation to that grand feast. The messengers are crossing mountains, and rivers, and deserts, and going to the four corners of the earth to invite every creature to be present; and God doesn't want one to be absent; He wants us all there. Man gets up a feast, and what a rush there is to get the best seat; but God prepares His feast, and there are empty chairs. Men begin to send in excuses.

They fast rain in upon Him. Christ has not only to provide a feast, but also to fill the chairs. "I pray thee have me excused."

A SOLEMN THOUGHT

Did you ever stop to think what would take place in a city like London if God should take every man and woman at their word, and just excuse them, and with one stroke clasp them all in the arms of death? I don't think there would be such a crowd here tomorrow night if that should take place within the next twenty-four hours. A good many of the congregation would be absent. All you people that are making excuses, you would be gone.

How many of you? If I should go down to the audience I would find that every one that is not already saved would have an excuse. You would have an excuse right on the end of your tongue; and if you haven't one already, Satan would be ready to help you to make one. That has been his business for the last 6,000 years - making excuses. "With one consent they begin to make excuse." It would be a very strange thing that would take place, if every man and woman in this great city should be excused, and God should just take them right away. There would be no drunkards reeling along on your streets tomorrow, for I never heard of a drunkard yet that didn't want to be excused. If he accepts the invitation, he must give up the rum-bowl. No drunkards shall enter the kingdom of heaven; there will be none at the marriage supper of the Lamb. A good many publicans would be gone, if not all of them. They would want to give up their businesses. But they say, "We didn't want to give up our businesses," and they go on in their hellish traffic, destroying the bodies and souls of men. A good many cabmen would be absent tomorrow; there wouldn't be so many cabs in the streets of London, because, if they accepted this invitation, they would have to give up their Sunday business. A good many merchants and shopkeepers would not be here tomorrow. They want to be excused. They say they are too busy, and haven't time to accept this invitation.

EXCUSED FROM WHAT?

Well, the friends that are making excuses just stop now and think a little; and would you just ask yourselves what you are being excused from? From heaven; from the society of the pure; those that have "washed their robes and made them white in the blood of the Lamb"; those that have been gathering for the last 6,000 years from the time that Abel went up, all along down to the present time, while the best of earth are not down here; they are in heaven. And when man says, "I pray thee, have me excused," it really means he doesn't want to be there. He wants to be excused from those mansions that Christ is preparing for those that love Him: they want to be excused from the society of angels and the society of God the Father, Christ the Son, and God the Holy Ghost; they want to be excused from the society of the redeemed ones that have already gone up on high.

Now, I can't speak for the rest of you, but if I know my own heart tonight, I would rather be torn from limb to limb on this platform, rather have my heart torn out of my body before I leave the platform, than to be absent from the marriage supper of the Lamb. I would ten thousand times rather die tonight, and be sure of meeting with the blessed and the purified in yon world of light than to live a hundred years and have the wealth of the world rolled at my feet, and then die and miss that wonderful scene. I have missed a good many appointments, but by the grace of God I want to make that one; I want to be at the marriage supper of the Lamb. Blessed is he that shall be at the marriage supper of the Lamb.

What a glorious thing it would be if every man and woman in this audience would give up all their excuses tonight! It is said, "God's hail shall sweep away those refuges of lies." Someone has said, "Let some plague strike you, and half your excuse is gone." Let death give you one look, and the other half is gone. When we come down to the gate of death, how these excuses will blow away in the dim past!

THE ORIGIN OF EXCUSES

You know the origin, don't you, of excuses? Why, they are as old as man himself. No sooner had Adam fallen than God came down to find him with an excuse. Satan was there, and he helped Adam to make the excuse. Adam said, "It was this woman you gave me." He turned it back on God really, and Eve laid it on Satan; and so all Adam's children have been making excuses ever since; they are very good at it.

THE LANDOWNER'S CASTLE

Let us look at the excuses those other men made. One man "bought a piece of land," and he must go and see it. A strange time to go and see land at suppertime! He ought to have gone in the morning, at breakfast time. As someone has said, if he had been a good businessman, he would have gone and looked at it before he bought it. But now he had bought it, no one could steal the land and run off with it in his pocket. It was not that he had not got the title of it, or that someone had got another deed and that he lost the title of his land. Was it going to make his land any better by looking at it? Would it improve it by looking at it? There is not a person in this hall but says that on the face of it, it was a lie. That is what it was. That little boy down there says that it was. The man says to the servant, "I will be happy to be at your feast, but I must go and look at my land, and you will excuse me." That is how people talk now. I want to go to heaven; there is no one wants to be saved more than I do, but I don't know the way. You should find the way, if you are in earnest, into the kingdom of God.

ANOTHER LIE

What is the next man's excuse? "I have bought five yoke of oxen, and I go to prove them." Why didn't he do so before he bought them? He could let his oxen stand in the stall until he accepted this invitation; but no; he must needs go and prove his oxen right at that very minute, just at suppertime; - a queer time to prove oxen - but he must needs go right off then to prove his oxen; and away he went. Another lie. You know it. There's not a man or woman here that's making excuse but will say it is a lie on the face of it. That wasn't the reason he didn't want to go. It is like people now. They don't believe the Gospel is good news; they don't believe that the Gospel is glad tidings; they don't believe that the Gospel is peace and joy.

THE MARRIED MAN'S EXCUSE

The next man's excuse, someone has said, was more absurd than the other two. He married a wife and couldn't come? Why didn't he take his wife with him? Who likes to go to a feast more than a young bride? But the invitation is to the whole family, not one left out. And then, if his wife didn't go with him, she would stay at home and let him accept the invitation. He might have left her at home to go to that feast; but the fact was he didn't want to go; it was a manufactured excuse. That is what Satan is doing, rocking people off to sleep in the cradle of excuses. May God wake you tonight that these excuses may flee away!

When you come before God not one of these excuses given would stand the light of eternity. Not one of them would a man stand up and give to God. Eighteen hundred years have rolled away, and *have men grown wiser?*

Have men got any better excuse today? Can you find any better excuse now right down in that hall tonight? If I ask that young lady what her excuse is, would she have a better one than that man had? Yon grey-haired man might be asked why he didn't accept the invitation - would he have any better reason? If I go to that young man in the gallery, and ask him what his excuse is, and why he didn't accept of this invitation, could he give a better one?

Now I have met with a great many people, and talked to them about their souls; and in all my travels I never found a man who had a better excuse than these three. When you analyse and look them over, you see they look absurd, don't they?

Come now, my friends, let us *look at your excuses.*

What are they? Let me take up some I find every night in the inquiry room. Only last night I found one very anxious to be saved, but "it was such a hard thing to be a Christian." God, in other words, they meant, was a hard Master, and really they meant that Satan was an easy one. Now is that true? The best witness to testify in a court to the character of two masters would be he that had served those masters. If I had worked for two men, I could tell more about them than a man that hadn't worked for the two, couldn't I? Now, if you have worked for Satan and haven't worked for the Lord, if you have been a servant of Satan and haven't been a servant of the Lord Jesus, I contend you don't know anything about it, and you can't say He is a hard Master. No one can say God is a hard Master until they have been in His service. Now if I could summon up witnesses tonight that have been in the service of Satan and the service of the Lord Jesus, I contend there would not be a man that would rise in this audience and say, "I have found God a hard Master."

THE DEVIL A HARD MASTER

If I should ask the disciples of Jesus Christ tonight to speak out in this hall, would they say they found God a hard Master? Is it true, O disciples of the Lord Jesus, that He is a hard Master and the devil is an easy one? (Cries of "No") What do you say? (Repeated cries of "No.") Hear the witnesses say it. They say "No." Let me ask you another question. "Is not the devil a hard master?" (Loud cries of "Yes.") "Who is the easiest master to serve?" (A number of voices, "Christ.") Not only that, my friends, but I will take the bitterest enemies Christianity has got here in London, and I might bring them up to this platform tonight and they would testify themselves that the devil is a hard master.

In New York City there is a little iron bridge running from the police court, as we call it, where the men are tried; and on one side of the bridge is written, *"The Bridge of Sighs", and* on the other, written in iron letters, *"The way of the transgressors is hard."* I said to the officer of the prison, "What made you put that up there?" "Why," he says, "there is not a man that goes over that bridge that does not go weeping, and therefore we call it 'The Bridge of Sighs.' "Now, you go to the prison and ask the convict if he has not found the way of the transgressors hard. Ask the man who has been in prison ten years, and who has to be there ten years longer, if he hasn't found the service of Satan hard, if he hasn't found him to be a bad master." What did the Lord Jesus say to Saul? "Saul, Saul! It is hard for thee to kick against the pricks." It is hard for *"thee"* - not hard for the Lord Jesus - but it was hard for Saul. It is hard for a man to contend with his Maker. It is hard for a man to fight against God. But I will tell you why you found the way hard. It is because you have been trying to serve God in the flesh; it is because you have been trying to serve God with the old carnal heart, which is enmity against God and is not subject to the law of God. No man can serve God until he is born of the Spirit; and then the "yoke is easy," then the "burden is light," and then God is an easy Master.

I tried to serve God in the flesh. I tried and failed; and it was hard to be a Christian; but when God snapped the fetters and set free my captive soul, and when I was born of the Spirit, the "yoke was easy and the burden was light." I stand here tonight to testify of the Lord Jesus Christ that He is *An Easy Master.*

He is not a hard Master; His yoke is easy and His burden is light. All His ways are ways of pleasantness. It is a delightful journey if you have Christ with you; but if you reject Him, and try to serve God without Christ, you will find it hard and dark and utterly impossible. So don't go out of here tonight and say God is a hard Master and Satan is an easy one. If you believe it, go and ask that drunkard who has been a drunkard for the last ten years. Go down to his home. It is a little hell upon earth. Oh, how dark and gloomy that drunkard's home is! Ask that drunkard if he has found the devil an easy master, and he will tell you that it is hard and dark; not only that, it grows darker and darker, and harder and harder as he journeys on. And if you could go down to the lost world and summon up one that has been there for the last thousand years to come up from the infernal pit - the dark caverns of hell - to tell you of his woe and his agony, he would tell you it is not only hard in this life, but ten times harder in the life to come. But go and ask that humble disciple of the Lord Jesus that has been walking with Christ for the last twenty years. Let him come up to this platform. See his eye, and there is pure light from Calvary shining across his path, and the light of Calvary is flashing around his countenance. Let that man tell of the peace and the joy he has in the service of Christ - how the way is lighter and lighter as he journeys on, and his hopes brighter and brighter as he comes nearer his eternal home, Nay, if we could go up to glory and bring down one that has been there for the last thousand years, if he should come from that world of light and tell of the joy, and the peace, and the glory of the upper world, oh, my friends, then you would find that there is a difference between him who serves Satan and him who serves the Lord Jesus.

So, my friends, don't go away from here tonight and say God is a hard Master and Satan an easy one; for Satan is a liar, and he has deceived the whole human race. *Tonight Change Masters:* make up your mind you will accept of the invitation to be present at the marriage supper of the Lamb. But a man over there says, "Mr. Moody, that is not my case at all - not my excuse. My excuse is, I don't know as I am elected. If I were, I would make sure of salvation; but I don't know I am one of the elect." Now, I won't give any uncertain sound on this point. I won't say that no unconverted man in London has nothing to do with the doctrine of election. Now, bear that in mind. You have no more to do with the doctrine of election than you have with the Government of China: not a bit more. Now then, what else? Suppose I am walking down by the Agricultural Hall tonight, and I see the people going in; I step up to a policeman and say, "Who is invited to that meeting?" and the policeman says, "No one is invited except those that have tickets." I have no ticket, therefore I can't go in. I go down to another hall, and see people crowding in, and I find there is a lecture, but no one is admitted there but those that belong to the society. I don't belong to the society, and can't get in. I find there is another meeting; but none are admitted but women. I am not a woman, and can't go in. I go on a little further, and find a public meeting. I make inquiries, and find it is a club, and none but those belonging to the club can go in. I can't go in there. I come to another building, and I find written up on its front, in great letters of fire, *"Whosoever Will, Come In"* and in I go - that's me. That's the way God puts His proclamation "Whosoever will, let him come in from the highways and the hedges, the blind, the lame, the halt, the deaf, the dumb, the sick - rich and poor all alike, come to the feast, and come just as you are."

Well, then, you say, what am I to do with that observation about election? Get into the Church, and we will talk to you about that. I am talking now to those who are not in the Church. You must deal with that word "whosoever" before you deal with election. That must come first. When you begin to read you must begin with the alphabet. You don't commence with the first reader: you must commence at once with the ABC; and if you are to learn arithmetic, you don't commence with geometry or algebra, you commence clear on at the beginning; and if you want to go into God's kingdom, you must go in God's way; and "whosoever will," let him go, and after you have got in we will talk to you about election. It will be time enough to talk about it then.

I don't know if it is true, but I have thought that after the Lord Jesus had gone to heaven, and Paul read that epistle he saw how some people would go and tumble over it, and perhaps he would look down to London here in the afternoon of the 19th century, and he would see how some people would give an excuse for not going to the feast. Whether He came down or caught up John, I don't know which; but John and the Master came together again. He was "in the spirit" on Patmos "on the Lord's day." Now John wrote these things to the churches, and he took up a pen, and kept on and on writing; and before he closed the book the Master said, "John, write this: 'The Spirit and the Bride say, Come. And let him that heareth say, Come'" and I can imagine he would say, "There are some that can't hear" "Well, let him that is athirst come." Some will say, "I am not willing, and not authorized." But it is broader still, "Whosoever *will,* let him take of the water of life freely." Isn't that broad enough? If God says, "Let him take," all the devils in hell could not stop you. "I will take the cup of salvation, and call upon the name of the Lord." Who will take the cup tonight? Who will take salvation as the gift tonight? Who will accept of the invitation to be present at the marriage supper of the Lamb tonight? Never mind about election, my friends. The invitation is to the broad, broad world. "Go ye into the world, and preach the Gospel to every creature." That means every one here. Will you believe the Gospel, and be saved? Will you accept of the invitation tonight? Oh, may God help you this night and this hour to accept of the invitation to be at the marriage supper of the Lamb!

Ah! But I can imagine those young people sending in their excuse. They are not troubled about election, not troubled at all with that excuse; but their excuse is this: if they become Christians, they will have to *Give Up All Pleasure* and all joy; they will have to put on a long face, and walk right straight through the world, and have no more joy, no more pleasure until they get to heaven. That kept me away from Christ for years. I used to think I should like to die a lingering disease, to know when death was coming, and before I died I would become a Christian, and get to heaven, making the most of both worlds, enjoying this world, and enjoying the world to come. I thought if I became a Christian, I should have to give up all true pleasure and all true joy until I got to heaven. There was never a greater lie told in hell or on earth than that. Does it make a man gloomy to become an heir of heaven? Does it make a man gloomy to become a child of the Lord, and to have the great God look down from His throne in heaven, and say, "That is My son; I have set My love upon him. That is My daughter!"

THE ONLY SOURCE OF JOY

Why, there is a man on his way to the execution. In a few minutes his soul is to be launched into eternity! See him tremble from head to foot when he is being led out to execution! Flash across the wires comes a message from the Queen. She sends a reprieve, and I run in haste and take it to the condemned man, and say, "Good news! You haven't to die. Here is a reprieve from the Queen." Is that to make him gloomy? Is that to give a man a long face? Here is a man dying for want of water, and I go and give him a tumbler of clear crystal water. Is that to make him gloomy? Christ is the Water of Life. Here is a man dying for want of bread, and I give him bread. Is that to make him gloomy? That is what Christ is; He is the Bread of Life. Why should it make me gloomy to get an invitation to a feast? When my little children get an invitation to go to a party, I am not long in the house before I hear of it. My little boy claps his hands with glee, and jumps for joy. That little girl down there likes to go to a party - to a feast. My little child, I have got an invitation for you; God wants you to go to the marriage supper of the Lamb. You are invited, little child - mother too; come along; all are invited. All ye young people come to Christ tonight. Make haste and accept of this invitation. Don't believe Satan's lies any longer that it makes a man gloomy to be a follower of the Lord Jesus Christ. Men are gloomy for the want of Christ. All the trouble in this world is because men have rejected Christ and salvation.

Then there is another excuse I heard from a man in the inquiry-room the other night. "I should like to go to Christ, but God will not receive me." "Why not?" "Because I am such a sinner." "You don't know God. If you did, you wouldn't talk in that way."

HE RECEIVETH SINNERS

"This man receiveth sinners and eateth with them." O sinner! Come along tonight. I don't care who you are or what your past life has been. It may be as black as hell itself, but "the blood of Jesus Christ cleanseth from all sin." He will clothe you with His own garment, and bring you into His banqueting house, and the banner over you will be Love. It may be I have been speaking to some poor prodigal who has been strolling along the streets for the last few weeks, who saw the crowd going into the Agricultural Hall, and was drifted along into this hall. Perhaps his mother is dead and in her grave; perhaps the father has cast him off because he is a prodigal, a wanderer, and a drunkard, and he says to himself, "Nobody cares for my soul. There's no eye on earth to pity me, no hand reached out to help me."

O prodigal! If you are here tonight, I bring you good news. I have an invitation to you from the King of kings - the Lord of Glory.

He wants you to go to the marriage supper of His own Son. You are invited tonight as much as any king or prince that has ever lived, and you are as precious in the sight of God as any soul in London. Come now, just as you are. Don't wait another minute. Say now, "By the grace of God I will accept the offer of the invitation; I will be at the marriage supper of the Lamb. If the Lord Jesus will receive me, He will have me." My dear friends, I tell you He *will* receive you. I challenge any man that ever was upon the face of the earth to say that when he came to Christ, Christ didn't receive him. Did you ever hear of such a case? Did you ever read of such a case? That has never happened yet. "Him that cometh unto me I will in no wise cast out," says the Son of God. Those are the words of Christ, and He *will* receive you.

I wish I could tell you how willing He is; I wish I could tell you how He is longing to receive every soul here, and that He will never "see of the travail of His soul and be satisfied" until sinners come flocking to Him. What He wants is to give life. What He wants is to bless. What He wants is to receive. Why! There is joy in heaven over one sinner that repenteth. If there should be thousands here who repent tonight, what joy there would be in heaven! What a shout around the throne! How they would lift high their hallelujahs, and sing tonight sweeter than they have sung for many a night, if there is a great rush into the kingdom of God. Oh, may God lead you to accept the invitation; and if you go, He will receive you.

A CHAPTER OF AUTOBIOGRAPHY

Let me tell you a little incident that happened in our own family to illustrate God's willingness to receive sinners. The first thing I remember in my life was the death of my father. He died before I was four years old. One beautiful day in June he fell suddenly dead on the floor, and his sudden death gave me such a shock that I have never forgotten it. It made an impression on my young mind that followed me through life. I can't remember the funeral. The only thing I remember of my father was his sudden death. The next thing I remember was that my mother was laid away upon a sick bed; and the third thing - for afflictions don't come generally singly - was that my oldest brother became a prodigal and ran away. I well remember how that Mother mourned for that boy. I well remember away back in my early childhood how that mother thought of that boy, and I used to think Mother loved him more than all the rest of us put together - and I think she did; it was the love of pity. I remember the cold winter nights, as we used to sit round the old family fireside, and we talked to our mother about our father -how he acted and what he used to do, and we would sit for hours and hear Mother talk of him; but if we mentioned that elder brother all would be silent. Mother never heard his name mentioned without tears coming; and some nights when there would be gales of wind, Mother didn't sleep at all. She thought, "He may be on the sea, and in that gale. He may be in trouble," and these nights she was ever praying for him.

THE MOTHER'S CRY

I remember some nights waking past midnight and hearing a voice in my mother's chamber; and I heard that mother weeping and saying, "O God, send back my boy. O God, shelter him and protect him, and take care of him." That was her cry. And when there came a day when the nation returned thanks for the harvest, a day when all the family came together, Mother used to say to us and raise our hopes, "Perhaps he will come back today," and his chair was kept vacant, and the place at the table. And yet he never returned. We wrote to different parts of the country as we grew up. If we found any paper that had a man named with the name of our brother, we would write to see if it was our brother. I remember once finding a notice in a Californian paper of a man bearing that name, and I thought it was him. I wrote out there, and was very disappointed at receiving a letter telling me he wasn't the man. Yet Mother prayed on and hoped on, seemingly against hope, until the hair once black turned grey, and the step once firm began to tremble, and I could see grief carrying that dear mother into an untimely grave. How my heart used to bleed for her!

THE PRODIGAL'S RETURN

One day, as she was sitting in her little cottage, her two youngest children, that were infants when brother left home, and were now grown up almost to manhood and womanhood, sitting at the table with her, a stranger appeared at the gate, and he came up to the east piazza and stood with his arms folded, looking on that mother he hadn't seen for years. Mother didn't recognize her boy; but when she saw those tears rolling down over the long black beard, through those tears she saw it was her long lost boy; and when she saw it was her lost boy she said, "Oh, my son, come in." And he says with his arms folded, "No, Mother; I will not come across your threshold until you forgive me." Sinner, do you believe she was ready to forgive him? She didn't wait for him to come in, but ran to the door, threw her arms around his neck and wept for joy. The dead was alive, the lost was found, the wanderer was come home, and the joy it gave that mother - I cannot tell it to you. None but the mother that had the prodigal boy can realize that mother's joy. I cannot tell you what joy it gave us as family; but it was nothing compared to the joy in heaven tonight, if you will only come home. Your Father wants you; and so come home this very night. He will receive every one of you if you will only come. May God help you to come now! May the Lord incline you to come, and you will find a warm welcome. He will give you a hearty response! Oh, may God incline you now to believe on the Lord Jesus Christ and to be saved!

HEAVEN AND WHO ARE THERE
Luke 10:20: '...*rejoice, because your names are written in heaven.*'

I WAS ON MY WAY TO A MEETING ONE NIGHT WITH A FRIEND, AND HE ASKED, AS WE WERE DRAWING NEAR the church, "Mr. Moody, what are you going to preach about?" "I am going to preach about Heaven," I said. I noticed a scowl passing over his face, and I said, "What makes you look so?" "Why, your subject of Heaven. What's the use of talking upon a subject that's all speculation? It's only wasting time on a subject about which you can only speculate." My answer to that friend was, "If the Lord doesn't want us to speak about Heaven, He would never have told us about such a place in the Scriptures; and, as Timothy says, 'All the Scriptures are given by inspiration, and all parts are profitable.'

There's no part of the Word of God that is not profitable, and I believe if men would read more carefully these Scriptures they would think more of Heaven. If we want to get men to fix their hearts and attention upon Heaven, we must get them to read more about it. Men who say that Heaven is a speculation have not read their Bibles. In the blessed Bible there are allusions scattered all through it. If I were to read to you all the passages upon Heaven from Genesis to Revelation, it would take me all night and tomorrow to do it. When I took some of the passages lately and showed them to a lady, "Why," said she, "I didn't think there was so much about Heaven in the Bible." If I were to go into a foreign land and spend my days there, I would like to know all about it; its climate, its inhabitants, their customs, their privileges, their government. I would find nothing about that land that would not interest me. Suppose you all were going away to Africa, to Germany, to China, and were going to make one of those places your home, and suppose that I had just come from one of those countries, how eagerly you would listen to what I had to say. I can imagine how the old, grey-haired men and the young men and the deaf would crowd around and put up their hands to learn something about it. But there is a country in which you are going to spend your whole future, and you are listless about what kind of a country it is. My friends, where are you going to spend eternity? Your life here is very brief. Life is but an inch of time; it is but a span, but a fibre, which will soon be snapped, and you will be ushered into eternity. Where are you going to spend it? If I were to ask you who were going to spend your eternity in Heaven to stand up, nearly everyone of you would rise. There is not a man here, not one in Chicago, who has not some hope of reaching Heaven. Now, if we are going to spend our future there, it becomes us to go to work and find out all about it. I call your attention to this truth that Heaven is just as much a place as Chicago. It is a destination - it is a locality. Some people say there is no Heaven. Some men will tell you this earth is all the heaven we have. Queer kind of heaven this. Look at the poverty, the disease in the city; look at the men out of employment walking around our streets, and then say this is Heaven. How low a man has got when he comes to think in this way. There is a land where the weary are at rest; there is a land where there is peace and joy - where no sorrow dwells, and as we think of it, and speak about it, how sweet it looms up before us.

I remember soon after I got converted, a pantheist got hold of me, and just tried to draw me back to the world. Those men who try to get hold of a young convert are the worst set of men. I don't know a worse man than he who tries to pull young Christians down. He is nearer the borders of hell than any man I know. When this man knew I had found Jesus he just tried to pull me down. He tried to argue with me, and I did not know the Bible very well then, and he got the best of me. The only way to get the best of those atheists, pantheists, or infidels is to have a good knowledge of the Bible. Well, this pantheist told me God was everywhere - in the air, in the sun, in the moon, in the earth, in the stars, but really he meant nowhere. And the next time I went to pray it seemed as if I was not praying anywhere or to anyone.

We have ample evidence in the Bible that there is such a place as Heaven, and we have abundant manifestation that His influence from Heaven is felt among us. He is not in person among us; only in spirit. The sun is 95,000,000 miles from the earth, yet we feel its rays. In Second Chronicles we read: "If my people, which are called by my name, shall humble themselves, and pray, and seek my face, and turn from their wicked ways; then will I hear from heaven, and will forgive their sin, and will heal their land." Here is one reference, and when it is read, a great many people might ask: "How far is Heaven away? Can you tell us that?" I don't know how far it is away, but there is one thing I can tell you. He can hear prayer as soon as the words are uttered. There has not been a prayer said that He has not heard; not a tear shed that He has not seen. We don't want to learn the distance. What we want to know is that God is there, and Scripture tells us that. Turn to First Kings and we read: "And hearken thou to the supplication of thy servant, and of thy people Israel, when they shall pray toward this place: and hear thou in heaven thy dwelling place: and when thou hearest, forgive." Now, it is clearly taught in the Word of God that the Father dwells there. It is His dwelling place, and in Acts we see that Jesus is there too. "But he, being full of the Holy Ghost, looked up steadfastly into heaven, and saw the glory of God, and Jesus standing on the right hand of God," and by the eye of faith we can see Him there tonight too. And by faith we shall be brought into His presence, and we shall be satisfied when we gaze upon Him. Stephen, when he was surrounded by the howling multitude, saw the Son of Man there, and when Jesus looked down upon earth and saw this first martyr in the midst of his persecutors, He looked down and gave him a welcome. We'll see Him by and by. It is not the jasper streets and golden gates that attract us to Heaven. What are your golden palaces on earth - what is it that makes them so sweet? It is the presence of some loving wife or fond children. Let them be taken away and the charm of your home is gone. And so it is Christ that is the charm of Heaven to the Christian. Yes, we shall see Him there. How sweet the thought that we shall dwell with Him forever, and shall see the nails in His hands and in His feet, which He received for us.

I read a little story not long since that went to my heart. A mother was on the point of death, and the child was taken away from her in case it would annoy her. It was crying continually to be taken to its mother, and teased the neighbours. By and by the mother died, and the neighbours thought it was better to bury the mother without letting the child see her dead face. They thought the sight of the dead mother would not do the child any good, and so they kept it away. When the mother was buried and the child was taken back to the house, the first thing she did was to run into her mother's sitting room and look all round it, and from there to the bedroom, but no mother was there, and she went all over the house crying, "Mother, Mother!" but the child could not find her, and coming to the neighbour, said: "Take me back, I don't want to stay here if I cannot see my Mother." It wasn't the home that made it so sweet to the child. It was the presence of the Mother. And so it is not Heaven that is alone attractive to us; it is the knowledge that Jesus, our leader, our brother, our Lord, is there.

And the spirits of loved ones, whose bodies we have laid in the earth, will be there. We shall be in good company there. When we reach that land we shall meet all the Christians who have gone before us. We are told in Matthew, too, that we shall meet angels there: "Take heed that ye despise not one of these little ones; for I say unto you, that in heaven their angels do always behold the face of my Father which is in heaven." Yes, the angels are there, and we shall see them when we get home.

He is there, and where He is, His disciples shall be, for He has said: "I go to prepare a place for you, that where I am, there ye may be also." I believe that when we die the spirit leaves the body and goes to the mansion above, and by and by the body will be resurrected and it shall see Jesus. Very often people come to me and say: "Mr. Moody, do you think we shall know each other in Heaven?" Very often it is a mother who has lost a dear child, and who wishes to see it again. Sometimes it is a child who has lost a mother, a father, and who wants to recognize them in Heaven. There is just one verse in Scripture in answer to this, and that is: "We shall be satisfied." It is all I want to know. My brother who went up there the other day I shall see, because I will be satisfied. We will see all those we loved on earth up there, and if we loved them here we will love them ten thousand times more when we meet them there.

Another thought. In the tenth chapter of Luke we are told our names are written there if we are Christians. Christ just called His disciples up and paired them off and sent them out to preach the Gospel. Two of us - Mr. Sankey and myself - going about and preaching the Gospel, are nothing new. You will find them away back eighteen hundred years ago, going off two by two, like Brothers Bliss and Whittle, and Brothers Needham and Stebbins, to different towns and villages. They had gone out, and there had been great revivals in all the cities, towns, and villages they had entered. Everywhere they had met with the greatest success. Even the very devils were subject to them. Disease had fled before them. When they met a lame man they said to him, "You don't want to be lame any longer," and he walked. When they met a blind man they but told him to open his eyes, and behold, he could see. And they came to Christ and rejoiced over their great success, and He just said to them, "I will give you something to rejoice over. Rejoice that your names are written in Heaven." Now there are a great many people who do not believe in such an assurance as this: "Rejoice, because your names are written in heaven." How are you going to rejoice if your names are not written there? While speaking about this some time ago, a man told me we were preaching a very ridiculous doctrine when we preached this doctrine of assurance. I ask you in all candour, what are you going to do with this assurance if we don't preach it? It is stated that our names are written there; blotted out of the Book of Death and transferred to the Book of Life.

I remember, while in Europe, I was travelling with a friend - she is in this hall tonight. On one occasion, we were journeying from

London to Liverpool, and the question was put as to where we would stop. We said we would go to the North Western, at Lime Street, as that was the hotel where Americans generally stopped at. When we got there the house was full; they could not let us in. Every room was engaged. But this friend said, "I am going to stay here, I engaged a room ahead. I sent a telegram on." My friends, that is just what the Christians are doing - sending their names in ahead. They are sending a message up saying: "Lord Jesus, I want one of those mansions You are preparing; I want to be there." That's what they're doing. And every man and woman here, who wants one, if you have not already got one, had better make up your mind. Send your names up now. I would rather a thousand times have my name written in the Lamb's Book than have all the wealth of the world rolling at my feet. A man may get station in this world - it will fade away; he may get wealth, but it will prove a bauble - "What shall it profit a man if he gain the whole world and lose his own soul?" It is a solemn question, and let it go around the hall tonight: "Is my name written in the Book of Life?" I can imagine that man down there saying, "Yes; I belong to the Presbyterian Church; my name's on the church's books." It may be, but God keeps His books in a different fashion than that in which the church records of this city are kept. You may belong to a good many churches; you may be an elder or a deacon, and be a bright light in your Church, and yet you may not have your name written in the Book of Life. Judas was one of the twelve, and yet he hadn't his name written in the Book of Life. Satan was among the elect - he dwelt among the angels, and yet he was cast from the high hallelujahs. Is your name written in the Book of Life? A man told me, while speaking upon this subject, "That is all nonsense you are speaking." And a great many men here are of the same opinion; but I would like them to turn to Daniel, twelfth chapter, "And there shall be a time of trouble, such as never was since there was a nation even to that same time: and at that time thy people shall be delivered, every one that shall be found written in the book." Everyone shall be delivered whose names shall be found written in the Book. And we find Paul, in the letters that he wrote to the Philippians, addressing them as those "dear yokefellows, whose names were written in the Book of Life." If it is not our privilege to know that our names are written in the Book of Life, here is Paul sending greetings to his yokefellows, "whose names were written in the Book." Let us not be deceived in this. We see it too plainly throughout the Holy Word. In the chapter of Revelation which we have just read, we have three different passages referring to it, and in the twenty-seventh verse, almost the last words in the Scriptures, we read: "And there shall in no wise enter into it any thing that defileth, neither whatsoever worketh abomination, or maketh a lie: but they which are written in the Lamb's book of life." My friends, you will never see that city unless your names are written in that Book of Life. It is a solemn truth. Let it go home to every one, and sink into the hearts of all here tonight. Don't build your hopes on a false foundation; don't build your hopes on an empty profession. Be sure your name is written there. And the next thing, after your own names are written there, is to see that the names of the children God has given you are recorded there. Let the fathers and mothers assembled tonight hear this and take it to their hearts. See that your children's names are there. Ask your conscience if the name of your John, your Willie, your Mary, and your Alice - ask yourselves whether their names are recorded in the Book of Life. If not, make it the business of your life, rather than to pile up wealth for them; make it the one object of your existence to secure for them eternal life, rather than to pave the way to their death and ruin.

I read some time ago of a mother in an Eastern city who was stricken with consumption. At her dying hour she requested her husband to bring the children to her. The oldest one was brought first, and she laid her hand on his head and gave him her blessing and dying message. The next one was brought, and she gave him the same; and one after another came to her bedside until the little infant was brought in. She took it and pressed it to her bosom, and the people in the room, fearing that she was straining her strength, took the child away from her. As this was done she turned to the husband and said, "I charge you, sir, bring all those children home with you." And so God charges us. The promise is to us and to our children. We can have our names written there, and then, by the grace of God, we can call our children to us and know that their names are also recorded there. That great roll is being called, and those bearing the names are summoned every day - every hour; that great roll is being called tonight, and if your name were shouted, could you answer with joy? You have heard of a soldier who fell in our war. While he lay dying, he was heard to cry, "Here! Here!" Some of his comrades went up to him, thinking he wanted water, but he said, "They are calling the roll of Heaven, and I am answering," and in a faint voice he whispered "Here!" and passed away to Heaven. If that roll were called tonight, would you be ready to answer, "Here!" I am afraid not. Let us wake up; may every child of God wake up tonight. There is work to do. Fathers and mothers, look to your children. If I could only speak to one class, I would preach to parents, and try to show them the great responsibility that rests upon them - try to teach them how much more they should devote their lives to secure the immortal treasure of Heaven for their children, than to spend their lives in scraping together worldly goods for them.

There is a man living on the bank of the Mississippi River. The world calls him rich, but if he could call back his first-born son he would give up all his wealth. The boy was brought home one day unconscious. When the doctor examined him he turned to the father, who stood at the bedside, and said, "There is no hope." "What!" exclaimed the father. "Is it possible my boy has got to die?" "There is no hope," replied the doctor. "Will he not come to?" asked the father. "He may resume consciousness, but he cannot live." "Try all your skill, doctor; I don't want my boy to die." By and by the boy regained a glimmering of consciousness, and when he was told that his death was approaching, he said to his father, "Won't you pray for my lost soul, father? You have never prayed for me." The old man wept. It was true. During the seventeen years that God had given him his boy he had never spent an hour in prayer for his soul, but the object of his life had been to accumulate wealth for that first-born. Am I speaking to a prayerless father or mother tonight? Settle the question of your soul's salvation and pray for the son or daughter God has given you.

But I have another anecdote to tell. It was Ralph Wells who told me of this one. A certain gentleman had been a member of the Presbyterian Church. His little boy was sick. When he went home his wife was weeping, and she said, "Our boy is dying. He has had a change for the worse. I wish you would go in and see him." The father went into the room and placed his hand on the brow of his dying boy, and could feel that the cold, damp sweat was gathering there; that the cold, icy hand of death was feeling for the cords of life. "Do you know, my boy, that you are dying?" asked the father. "Am I? Is this death? Do you really think I am dying?" "Yes, my son, your end on earth is near." "And will I be with Jesus tonight, father?" "Yes, you will be with the Saviour." "Father, don't you weep, for when I get there I will go straight to Jesus and tell Him you have been trying all my life to lead me to Him." God has given me two little children, and ever since I can remember I have directed them to Christ, and I would rather they carried this message to Jesus - that I had tried all my life to lead them to Him - than have all the crowns of the earth; and I would rather lead them to Jesus than give them the wealth of the world. If you have got a child, go and point the way: I challenge any man to speak of Heaven without speaking of children. "For of such is the kingdom of heaven." Fathers and mothers and professed Christians ignore this sometimes. They go along themselves and never try to get any to Heaven with them. Let us see to this at once, and let us pray that there may be many names written in the Lamb's Book of Life tonight.

6

WHY GOD USED D. L. MOODY

A SERMON BY R. A. TORREY

❧

WHY GOD USED D. L. MOODY

The Rev. R. A. Torrey, a graduate of Yale College and Divinity School and a Congregational minister, was personally selected by Mr. Moody for the post of superintendent to the newly formed 'Bible Institute of the Chicago Evangelisation Society' (later to become Moody Bible Institute). Moody and Torrey were very much opposites and one co-worker, describing the two men said, "Moody was brusque, impulsive and uneducated; Torrey was polished, logical and scholarly."

In 1923, Torrey wrote a brief and informative booklet called 'Why God Used D. L. Moody'. He drew seven challenging lessons from the life of his friend Moody, which are included as a closing chapter to this D. L. Moody treasury.

God is still looking for men and women who like Moody aspired to be used by God in His service in the evangelisation of the world.

SERMON BY R.A. TORREY – 1923

Eighty-six years ago (February 5, 1837), there was born of poor parents in a humble farmhouse in Northfield, Massachusetts, a little baby who was to become the greatest man, as I believe, of his generation or of his century — Dwight L. Moody. After our great generals, great statesmen, great scientists and great men of letters have passed away and been forgotten, and their work and its helpful influence has come to an end, the work of D. L. Moody will go on and its saving influence continue and increase, bringing blessing not only to every state in the Union but to every nation on earth. Yes, it will continue throughout the ages of eternity.

My subject is "Why God Used D. L. Moody," and I can think of no subject upon which I would rather speak. For I shall not seek to glorify Mr. Moody, but the God who by His grace, His entirely unmerited favour, used him so mightily, and the Christ who saved him by His atoning death and resurrection life, and the Holy Spirit who lived in him and wrought through him and who alone made him the mighty power that he was to this world. Furthermore: I hope to make it clear that the God who used D. L. Moody in his day is just as ready to use you and me, in this day, if we, on our part, do what D. L. Moody did, which was what made it possible for God to so abundantly use him.

The whole secret of why D. L. Moody was such a mightily used man you will find in Psalm 62:11: "God hath spoken once; twice have I heard this; that POWER BELONGETH UNTO GOD." I am glad it does. I am glad that power did not belong to D. L. Moody; I am glad that it did not belong to Charles G. Finney; I am glad that it did not belong to Martin Luther; I am glad that it did not belong to any other Christian man whom God has greatly used in this world's history. Power belongs to God. If D. L. Moody had any power, and he had great power, he got it from God.

But God does not give His power arbitrarily. It is true that He gives it to whomsoever He will, but He wills to give it on certain conditions, which are clearly revealed in His Word; and D. L. Moody met those conditions and God made him the most wonderful preacher of his generation; yes, I think the most wonderful man of his generation.

But how was it that D. L. Moody had that power of God so wonderfully manifested in his life? Pondering this question it seemed to me that there were seven things in the life of D. L. Moody that accounted for God's using him so largely as He did.

(1) A FULLY SURRENDERED MAN

The first thing that accounts for God's using D. L. Moody so mightily was that he was a fully surrendered man. Every ounce of that two-hundred-and-eighty-pound body of his belonged to God; everything he was and everything he had, belonged wholly to God. Now, I am not saying that Mr. Moody was perfect; he was not. If I attempted to, I presume I could point out some defects in his character. It does not occur to me at this moment what they were; but I am confident that I could think of some, if I tried real hard. I have never yet met a perfect man, not one. I have known perfect men in the sense in which the Bible commands us to be perfect, i.e., men who are wholly God's, out and out for God, fully surrendered to God, with no will but God's will; but I have never known a man in whom I could not see some defects, some places where he might have been improved.

No, Mr. Moody was not a faultless man. If he had any flaws in his character, and he had, I presume I was in a position to know them better than almost any other man, because of my very close association with him in the later years of his life; and furthermore, I suppose that in his latter days he opened his heart to me more fully than to anyone else in the world. I think He told me some things that he told no one else. I presume I knew whatever defects there were in his character as well as anybody. But while I recognized such flaws, nevertheless, I know that he was a man who belonged wholly to God.

The first month I was in Chicago, we were having a talk about something upon which we very widely differed, and Mr. Moody turned to me very frankly and very kindly and said in defence of his own position: "Torrey, if I believed that God wanted me to jump out of that window, I would jump." I believe he would. If he thought God wanted him to do anything, he would do it. He belonged wholly, unreservedly, unqualifiedly, entirely, to God.

Henry Varley, a very intimate friend of Mr. Moody in the earlier days of his work, loved to tell how he once said to him: "It remains to be seen what God will do with a man who gives himself up wholly to Him." I am told that when Mr. Henry Varley said that, Mr. Moody said to himself: "Well, I will be that man." And I, for my part, do not think, "it remains to be seen" what God will do with a man who gives himself up wholly to Him. I think it has been seen already in D. L. Moody.

If you and I are to be used in our sphere as D. L. Moody was used in his, we must put all that we have and all that we are in the hands of God, for Him to use as He will, to send us where He will, for God to do with us what He will, and we, on our part, to do everything God bids us do.

There are thousands and tens of thousands of men and women in Christian work, brilliant men and women, rarely gifted men and women, men and women who are making great sacrifices, men and women who have put all conscious sin out of their lives, yet who, nevertheless, have stopped short of absolute surrender to God, and therefore have stopped short of fullness of power. But Mr. Moody did not stop short of absolute surrender to God; he was a wholly surrendered man, and if you and I are to be used, you and I must be wholly surrendered men and women.

(2) A MAN OF PRAYER

The second secret of the great power exhibited in Mr. Moody's life was that Mr. Moody was in the deepest and most meaningful sense a man of prayer. People oftentimes say to me: "Well, I went many miles to see and to hear D. L. Moody and he certainly was a wonderful preacher." Yes, D. L. Moody certainly was a wonderful preacher; taking it all in all, the most wonderful preacher I have ever heard, and it was a great privilege to hear him preach as he alone could preach; but out of a very intimate acquaintance with him I wish to testify that he was a far greater man of prayer than he was preacher.

Time and time again, he was confronted by obstacles that seemed insurmountable, but he always knew the way to surmount and to overcome all difficulties. He knew the way to bring to pass anything that needed to be brought to pass. He knew and believed in the deepest depths of his soul that "nothing was too hard for the Lord" and that prayer could do anything that God could do.

Often times Mr. Moody would write me when he was about to undertake some new work, saying: "I am beginning work in such and such a place on such and such a day; I wish you would get the students together for a day of fasting and prayer" And often I have taken those letters and read them to the students in the lecture room and said: "Mr. Moody wants us to have a day of fasting and prayer, first for God's blessing on our own souls and work, and then for God's blessing on him and his work."

Often we were gathered in the lecture room far into the night — sometimes till one, two, three, four or even five o'clock in the morning, crying to God, just because Mr. Moody urged us to wait upon God until we received His blessing. How many men and women I have known whose lives and characters have been transformed by those nights of prayer and who have wrought mighty things in many lands because of those nights of prayer!

One day Mr. Moody drove up to my house at Northfield and said: "Torrey, I want you to take a ride with me." I got into the carriage and we drove out toward Lover's Lane, talking about some great and unexpected difficulties that had arisen in regard to the work in Northfield and Chicago, and in connection with other work that was very dear to him.

As we drove along, some black storm clouds lay ahead of us, and then suddenly, as we were talking, it began to rain. He drove the horse into a shed near the entrance to Lover's Lane to shelter the horse, and then laid the reins upon the dashboard and said: "Torrey, pray"; and then, as best I could, I prayed, while he in his heart joined me in prayer. And when my voice was silent he began to pray. Oh, I wish you could have heard that prayer! I shall never forget it, so simple, so trustful, so definite and so direct and so mighty. When the storm was over and we drove back to town, the obstacles had been surmounted, and the work of the schools, and other work that was threatened, went on as it had never gone on before, and it has gone on until this day.

As we drove back, Mr. Moody said to me: "Torrey, we will let the other men do the talking and the criticizing, and we will stick to the work that God has given us to do, and let Him take care of the difficulties and answer the criticisms."

On one occasion Mr. Moody said to me in Chicago: "I have just found, to my surprise, that we are twenty thousand dollars behind in our finances for the work here and in Northfield, and we must have that twenty thousand dollars, and I am going to get it by prayer." He did not tell a soul who had the ability to give a penny of the twenty

WHY GOD USED D. L. MOODY

thousand deficit, but looked right to God and said: "I need twenty thousand dollars for my work; send me that money in such a way that I will know it comes straight from Thee." And God heard that prayer. The money came in such a way that it was clear that it came from God in direct answer to prayer.

Yes, D. L. Moody was a man who believed in the God who answers prayer, and not only believed in Him in a theoretical way but believed in Him in a practical way. He was a man who met every difficulty that stood in his way — by prayer. Everything he undertook was backed up by prayer, and in everything, his ultimate dependence was upon God.

(3) A DEEP AND PRACTICAL STUDENT OF THE BIBLE

The third secret of Mr. Moody's power, or the third reason why God used D. L. Moody, was because he was a deep and practical student of the Word of God. Nowadays it is often said of D. L. Moody that he was not a student. I wish to say that he was a student; most emphatically he was a student. He was not a student of psychology; he was not a student of anthropology — I am very sure he would not have known what that word meant; he was not a student of biology; he was not a student of philosophy; he was not even a student of theology, in the technical sense of the term; but he was a student, a profound and practical student of the one Book that is more worth studying than all other books in the world put together; he was a student of the Bible.

Every day of his life, I have reason for believing, he arose very early in the morning to study the Word of God, way down to the close of his life. Mr. Moody used to rise about four o'clock in the morning to study the Bible. He would say to me: "If I am going to get in any study, I have got to get up before the other folks get up"; and he would shut himself up in a remote room in his house, alone with his God and his Bible.

I shall never forget the first night I spent in his home. He had invited me to take the superintendency of the Bible Institute and I had already begun my work; I was on my way to some city in the East to preside at the International Christian Workers' Convention. He wrote me saying: "Just as soon as the Convention is over, come up to Northfield." He learned when I was likely to arrive and drove over to South Vernon to meet me. That night he had all the teachers from the Mount Hermon School and from the Northfield Seminary come together at the house to meet me, and to talk over the problems of the two schools. We talked together far on into the night, and then, after the principals and teachers of the schools had gone home, Mr. Moody and I talked together about the problems a while longer.

It was very late when I got to bed that night, but very early the next morning, about five o'clock, I heard a gentle tap on my door. Then I heard Mr. Moody's voice whispering: "Torrey, are you up?" I happened to be; I do not always get up at that early hour but I happened to be up that particular morning. He said: "I want you to go somewhere with me," and I went down with him. Then I found out that he had already been up an hour or two in his room studying the Word of God.

Oh, you may talk about power; but, if you neglect the one Book that God has given you as the one instrument through which He imparts and exercises His power, you will not have it. You may read many books and go to many conventions and you may have your all-night prayer meetings to pray for the power of the Holy Ghost; but unless you keep in constant and close association with the one Book, the Bible, you will not have power. And if you ever had power, you will not maintain it except by the daily, earnest, intense study of that Book.

Ninety-nine Christians in every hundred are merely playing at Bible study; and therefore ninety-nine Christians in every hundred are mere weaklings, when they might be giants, both in their Christian life and in their service.

It was largely because of his thorough knowledge of the Bible, and his practical knowledge of the Bible, that Mr. Moody drew such immense crowds. On "Chicago Day," in October 1893, none of the theatres of Chicago dared to open because it was expected that everybody in Chicago would go on that day to the World's Fair; and, in point of fact, something like four hundred thousand people did pass through the gates of the Fair that day. Everybody in Chicago was expected to be at that end of the city on that day. But Mr. Moody said to me: "Torrey, engage the Central Music Hall and announce meetings from nine o'clock in the morning till six o'clock at night." "Why," I replied, "Mr. Moody, nobody will be at this end of Chicago on that day; not even the theatres dare to open; everybody is going down to Jackson Park to the Fair; we cannot get anybody out on this day."

Mr. Moody replied: "You do as you are told"; and I did as I was told and engaged the Central Music Hall for continuous meetings from nine o'clock in the morning till six o'clock at night. But I did it with a heavy heart; I thought there would be poor audiences. I was on the program at noon that day. Being very busy in my office about the details of the campaign, I did not reach the Central Music Hall till almost noon. I thought I would have no trouble in getting in. But when I got almost to the Hall I found to my amazement that not only was it packed but the vestibule was packed and the steps were packed, and there was no getting anywhere near the door; and if I had not gone round and climbed in a back window they would have lost their speaker for that hour. But that would not have been of much importance, for the crowds had not gathered to hear me; it was the magic of Mr. Moody's name that had drawn them. And why did they long to hear Mr. Moody? Because they knew that while he was not versed in many of the philosophies and fads and fancies of the day, he did know the one Book that this old world most longs to know — the Bible.

I shall never forget Moody's last visit to Chicago. The ministers of Chicago had sent me to Cincinnati to invite him to come to

Chicago and hold a meeting. In response to the invitation, Mr. Moody said to me: "If you will hire the Auditorium for weekday mornings and afternoons and have meetings at ten in the morning and three in the afternoon, I will go." I replied: "Mr. Moody, you know what a busy city Chicago is, and how impossible it is for businessmen to get out at ten o'clock in the morning and three in the afternoon on working days. Will you not hold evening meetings and meetings on Sunday?" "No," he replied, "I am afraid if I did, I would interfere with the regular work of the churches."

I went back to Chicago and engaged the Auditorium, which at that time was the building having the largest seating capacity of any building in the city, seating in those days about seven thousand people; I announced weekday meetings, with Mr. Moody as the speaker, at ten o'clock in the mornings and three o'clock in the afternoons.

At once protests began to pour in upon me. One of them came from Marshall Field, at that time the business king of Chicago. "Mr. Torrey," Mr. Field wrote, "we businessmen of Chicago wish to hear Mr. Moody, and you know perfectly well how impossible it is for us to get out at ten o'clock in the morning and three o'clock in the afternoon; have evening meetings." I received many letters of a similar purport and wrote to Mr. Moody urging him to give us evening meetings. But Mr. Moody simply replied: "You do as you are told," and I did as I was told; that is the way I kept my job.

On the first morning of the meetings I went down to the Auditorium about half an hour before the appointed time, but I went with much fear and apprehension; I thought the Auditorium would be nowhere nearly full. When I reached there, to my amazement I found a queue of people four abreast extending from the Congress Street entrance to Wabash Avenue, then a block north on Wabash Avenue, then a break to let traffic through, and then another block, and so on. I went in through the back door, and there were many clamouring for entrance there. When the doors were opened at the appointed time, we had a cordon of twenty policemen to keep back the crowd; but the crowd was so great that it swept the cordon of policemen off their feet and packed eight thousand people into the building before we could get the doors shut. And I think there were as many left on the outside as there were in the building. I do not think that anyone else in the world could have drawn such a crowd at such a time.

Why? Because though Mr. Moody knew little about science or philosophy or literature in general, he did know the one Book that this old world is perishing to know and longing to know; and this old world will flock to hear men who know the Bible and preach the Bible as they will flock to hear nothing else on earth.

During all the months of the World's Fair in Chicago, no one could draw such crowds as Mr. Moody. Judging by the papers, one would have thought that the great religious event in Chicago at that time was the World's Congress of Religions. One very gifted man of letters in the East was invited to speak at this Congress. He saw in this invitation the opportunity of his life and prepared his paper, the exact title of which I do not now recall, but it was something along the line of "New Light on the Old Doctrines." He prepared the paper with great care, and then sent it around to his most trusted and gifted friends for criticisms. These men sent it back to him with such emendations as they had to suggest. Then he rewrote the paper, incorporating as many of the suggestions and criticisms as seemed wise. Then he sent it around for further criticisms. Then he wrote the paper a third time, and had it, as he trusted, perfect. He went on to Chicago to meet this coveted opportunity of speaking at the World's Congress of Religions.

It was at eleven o'clock on a Saturday morning (if I remember correctly) that he was to speak. He stood outside the door of the platform waiting for the great moment to arrive, and as the clock struck eleven he walked on to the platform to face a magnificent audience of eleven women and two men! But there was not a building anywhere in Chicago that would accommodate the very same day the crowds that would flock to hear Mr. Moody at any hour of the day or night.

Oh, men and women, if you wish to get an audience and wish to do that audience some good after you get them, study, study, STUDY the one Book, and preach, preach, PREACH the one Book, and teach, teach, TEACH the one Book, the Bible, the only Book that is God's Word, and the only Book that has power to gather and hold and bless the crowds for any great length of time.

(4) A HUMBLE MAN

The fourth reason why God continuously, through so many years, used D.L. Moody was because he was a humble man. I think D. L. Moody was the humblest man I ever knew in all my life. He loved to quote the words of another; "Faith gets the most; love works the most; but humility keeps the most."

He himself had the humility that keeps everything it gets. As I have already said, he was the most humble man I ever knew, i.e., the most humble man when we bear in mind the great things that he did, and the praise that was lavished upon him. Oh, how he loved to put himself in the background and put other men in the foreground. How often he would stand on a platform with some of us little fellows seated behind him and as he spoke he would say: "There are better men coming after me." As he said it, he would point back over his shoulder with his thumb to the "little fellows." I do not know how he could believe it, but he really did believe that the others that were coming after him were really better than he was. He made no pretence to a humility he did not possess. In his heart of hearts he constantly underestimated himself, and overestimated others.

He really believed that God would use other men in a larger measure than he had been used. Mr. Moody loved to keep himself in the background. At his conventions at Northfield, or anywhere else, he would push the other men to the front and, if he could, have them do all the preaching — McGregor, Campbell Morgan, Andrew Murray, and the rest of them. The only way we could get him to take any part in the program was to get up in the convention and move that we hear D. L. Moody at the next meeting. He continually put himself out of sight.

Oh, how many a man has been full of promise and God has used him, and then the man thought that he was the whole thing and God was compelled to set him aside! I believe more promising workers have gone on the rocks through self-sufficiency and self-esteem than through any other cause. I can look back for forty years, or more, and think of many men who are now wrecks or derelicts that at one time the world thought were going to be something great. But they have disappeared entirely from the public view. Why? Because of overestimation of self. Oh, the men and women who have been put aside because they began to think that they were somebody, that they were "it," and therefore God was compelled to set them aside.

I remember a man with whom I was closely associated in a great movement in this country. We were having a most successful convention in Buffalo, and he was greatly elated. As we walked down the street together to one of the meetings one day, he said to me: "Torrey, you and I are the most important men in Christian work in this country," or words to that effect. I replied: "John, I am sorry to hear you say that; for as I read my Bible I find man after man who had accomplished great things whom God had to set aside because of his sense of his own importance." And God set that man aside also from that time. I think he is still living, but no one ever hears of him, or has heard of him for years.

God used D. L. Moody, I think, beyond any man of his day; but it made no difference how much God used him, he never was puffed up. One day, speaking to me of a great New York preacher, now dead, Mr. Moody said: "He once did a very foolish thing, the most foolish thing that I ever knew a man, ordinarily so wise as he was, to do. He came up to me at the close of a little talk I had given and said:

'Young man, you have made a great address tonight.'" Then Mr. Moody continued: "How foolish of him to have said that! It almost turned my head." But, thank God, it did not turn his head, and even when pretty much all the ministers in England, Scotland and Ireland, and many of the English bishops were ready to follow D. L. Moody wherever he led, even then it never turned his head one bit. He would get down on his face before God, knowing he was human, and ask God to empty him of all self-sufficiency. And God did.

Oh, men and women! especially young men and young women, perhaps God is beginning to use you; very likely people are saying: "What a wonderful gift he has as a Bible teacher, what power he has as a preacher, for such a young man!" Listen: get down upon your face before God. I believe here lies one of the most dangerous snares of the Devil. When the Devil cannot discourage a man, he approaches him on another tack, which he knows is far worse in its results; he puffs him up by whispering in his ear: "You are the leading evangelist of the day. You are the man who will sweep everything before you. You are the coming man. You are the D. L. Moody of the day"; and if you listen to him, he will ruin you. The entire shore of the history of Christian workers is strewn with the wrecks of gallant vessels that were full of promise a few years ago, but these men became puffed up and were driven on the rocks by the wild winds of their own raging self-esteem.

(5) HIS ENTIRE FREEDOM FROM THE LOVE OF MONEY

The fifth secret of D. L. Moody's continual power and usefulness was his entire freedom from the love of money. Mr. Moody might have been a wealthy man, but money had no charms for him. He loved to gather money for God's work; he refused to accumulate money for himself. He told me during the World's Fair that if he had taken, for himself, the royalties on the hymnbooks, which he had published, they would have amounted, at that time, to a million dollars. But Mr. Moody refused to touch the money. He had a perfect right to take it, for he was responsible for the publication of the books and it was his money that went into the publication of the first of them.

Mr. Sankey had some hymns that he had taken with him to England and he wished to have them published. He went to a publisher (I think Morgan & Scott) and they declined to publish them, because, as they said, Philip Phillips had recently been over and published a hymnbook and it had not done well. However, Mr. Moody had a little money and he said that he would put it into the publication of these hymns in cheap form; and he did. The hymns had a most remarkable and unexpected sale; they were then published in book form and large profits accrued. The financial results were offered to Mr. Moody, but he refused to touch them. "But," it was urged on him, "the money belongs to you"; but he would not touch it.

Mr. Fleming H. Revell was at the time treasurer of the Chicago Avenue Church, commonly known as the Moody Tabernacle. Only the basement of this new church building had been completed, funds having been exhausted. Hearing of the hymnbook situation Mr. Revell suggested, in a letter to friends in London, that the money be given for completion of this building, and it was. Afterwards, so much money came in that it was given, by the committee, into whose hands Mr. Moody put the matter, to various Christian enterprises.

In a certain city to which Mr. Moody went in the latter years of his life, and where I went with him, it was publicly announced that Mr. Moody would accept no money whatever for his services. Now, in point of fact, Mr. Moody was dependent, in a measure, upon what was given him at various services; but when this announcement was made, Mr. Moody said nothing, and left that city without a penny's compensation for the hard work he did there; and, I think, he paid his own hotel bill. And yet a minister in that very city came out with an article in a paper, which I read, in which he told a fairy tale of the financial demands that Mr. Moody made upon them, which story I knew personally to be absolutely untrue. Millions of dollars passed into Mr. Moody hands, but they passed through; they did not stick to his fingers.

This is the point at which many an evangelist makes shipwreck, and his great work comes to an untimely end. The love of money on the part of some evangelists has done more to discredit evangelistic work in our day, and to lay many an evangelist on the shelf, than almost any other cause.

While I was away on my recent tour I was told by one of the most reliable ministers in one of our eastern cities of a campaign conducted by one who has been greatly used in the past. (Do not imagine, for a moment, that I am speaking of Billy Sunday, for I am not; this same minister spoke in the highest terms of Mr. Sunday and of a campaign that he conducted in a city where this minister was a pastor.) This evangelist of whom I now speak came to a city for a united evangelistic campaign and was supported by fifty-three churches. The minister who told me about the matter was himself chairman of the Finance Committee.

The evangelist showed such a longing for money and so deliberately violated the agreement he had made before coming to the city and so insisted upon money being gathered for him in other ways than he had himself prescribed in the original contract, that this minister threatened to resign from the Finance Committee. He was, however, persuaded to remain to avoid a scandal. "As the total result of the three weeks' campaign there were only twenty-four clear decisions," said my friend; "and after it was over the ministers got together and by a vote with but one dissenting voice, they agreed to send a letter to this evangelist telling him frankly that they were done with him and with his methods of evangelism forever, and that they felt it their duty to warn other cities against him and his methods and the results of his work." Let us lay the lesson to our hearts and take warning in time.

(6) HIS CONSUMING PASSION FOR THE SALVATION OF THE LOST

The sixth reason why God used D. L. Moody was because of his consuming passion for the salvation of the lost. Mr. Moody made the resolution, shortly after he himself was saved, that he would never let twenty-four hours pass over his head without speaking to at least one person about his soul. His was a very busy life, and sometimes he would forget his resolution until the last hour, and sometimes he would get out of bed, dress, go out and talk to someone about his soul in order that he might not let one day pass without having definitely told at least one of his fellow-mortals about his need and the Saviour who could meet it.

One night Mr. Moody was going home from his place of business. It was very late, and it suddenly occurred to him that he had not spoken to one single person that day about accepting Christ. He said to himself: "Here's a day lost. I have not spoken to anyone today and I shall not see anybody at this late hour." But as he walked up the street he saw a man standing under a lamppost. The man was a perfect stranger to him, though it turned out afterwards the man knew who Mr. Moody was. He stepped up to this stranger and said: "Are you a Christian?" The man replied: "That is none of your business, whether I am a Christian or not. If you were not a sort of a preacher I would knock you into the gutter for your impertinence." Mr. Moody said a few earnest words and passed on.

The next day that man called upon one of Mr. Moody's prominent business friends and said to him: "That man Moody of yours over on the North Side is doing more harm than he is good. He has got zeal without knowledge. He stepped up to me last night, a perfect stranger, and insulted me. He asked me if I were a Christian, and I told him it was none of his business and if he were not a sort of a preacher I would knock him into the gutter for his impertinence. He is doing more harm than he is good. He has got zeal without knowledge." Mr. Moody's friend sent for him and said: "Moody, you are doing more harm than you are good; you've got zeal without knowledge: you insulted a friend of mine on the street last night. You went up to him, a perfect stranger, and asked him if he were a Christian, and he tells me if you had not been a sort of a preacher he would have knocked you into the gutter for your impertinence. You are doing more harm than you are good; you have got zeal without knowledge."

Mr. Moody went out of that man's office somewhat crestfallen. He wondered if he were not doing more harm than he was good, if he really had zeal without knowledge. (Let me say, in passing, it is far better to have zeal without knowledge than it is to have knowledge without zeal. Some men and women are as full of knowledge as an egg is of meat; they are so deeply versed in Bible truth that they can sit in criticism on the preachers and give the preachers pointers, but they have so little zeal that they do not lead one soul to Christ in a whole year.)

Weeks passed by. One night Mr. Moody was in bed when he heard a tremendous pounding at his front door. He jumped out of bed and rushed to the door. He thought the house was on fire. He thought the man would break down the door. He opened the door and there stood this man. He said: "Mr. Moody, I have not had a good night's sleep since that night you spoke to me under the lamp-post, and I have come around at this unearthly hour of the night for you to tell me what I have to do to be saved." Mr. Moody took him in and told him what to do to be saved. Then he accepted Christ, and when the Civil War broke out, he went to the front and laid down his life fighting for his country.

Another night, Mr. Moody got home and had gone to bed before it occurred to him that he had not spoken to a soul that day about accepting Christ. "Well," he said to himself, "it is no good getting up now; there will be nobody on the street at this hour of the night." But he got up, dressed and went to the front door. It was pouring rain. "Oh," he said, "there will be no one out in this pouring rain.

Just then he heard the patter of a man's feet as he came down the street, holding an umbrella over his head. Then Mr. Moody darted out and rushed up to the man and said: "May I share the shelter of your umbrella?" "Certainly," the man replied. Then Mr. Moody said: "Have you any shelter in the time of storm?" and preached Jesus to him. Oh, men and women, if we were as full of zeal for the salvation of souls as that, how long would it be before the whole country would be shaken by the power of a mighty, God-sent revival?

One day in Chicago — the day after the elder Carter Harrison was shot, when his body was lying in state in the City Hall — Mr. Moody and I were riding up Randolph Street together in a streetcar right alongside of the City Hall. The car could scarcely get through because of the enormous crowds waiting to get in and view the body of Mayor Harrison. As the car tried to push its way through the crowd, Mr. Moody turned to me and said: "Torrey, what does this mean?" "Why," I said, "Carter Harrison's body lies there in the City Hall and these crowds are waiting to see it."

Then he said: "This will never do, to let these crowds get away from us without preaching to them; we must talk to them. You go and hire Hooley's Opera House (which was just opposite the City Hall) for the whole day." I did so. The meetings began at nine o'clock in the morning, and we had one continuous service from that hour until six in the evening, to reach those crowds.

Mr. Moody was a man on fire for God. Not only was he always "on the job" himself but he was always getting others to work as well. He once invited me down to Northfield to spend a month there with the schools, speaking first to one school and then crossing the river to the other. I was obliged to use the ferry a great deal; it was before the present bridge was built at that point.

One day he said to me: "Torrey, did you know that that ferryman that ferries you across every day was unconverted?" He did not tell me to speak to him, but I knew what he meant. When some days later it was told him that the ferryman was saved, he was exceedingly happy.

Once, when walking down a certain street in Chicago, Mr. Moody stepped up to a man, a perfect stranger to him, and said: "Sir, are you a Christian?" "You mind your own business," was the reply. Mr. Moody replied: "This is my business." The man said, "Well, then, you must be Moody." Out in Chicago they used to call him in those early days "Crazy Moody," because day and night he was speaking to everybody he got a chance to speak to about being saved.

One time he was going to Milwaukee, and in the seat that he had chosen sat a travelling man. Mr. Moody sat down beside him and immediately began to talk with him. " Where are you going?" Mr. Moody asked. When told the name of the town he said: "We will soon be there; we'll have to get down to business at once. Are you saved?" The man said that he was not, and Mr. Moody took out his Bible and there on the train showed him the way of salvation. Then he said: "Now, you must take Christ." The man did; he was converted right there on the train.

Most of you have heard, I presume, the story President Wilson used to tell about D. L. Moody. Ex-President Wilson said that he once went into a barbershop and took a chair next to the one in which D. L. Moody was sitting, though he did not know that Mr. Moody was there. He had not been in the chair very long before, as ex-President Wilson phrased it, he "knew there was a personality in the other chair," and he began to listen to the conversation going on; he heard Mr. Moody tell the barber about the Way of Life, and President Wilson said, "I have never forgotten that scene to this day." When Mr. Moody was gone, he asked the barber who he was; when he was told that it was D. L. Moody, President Wilson said: "It made an impression upon me I have not yet forgotten."

On one occasion in Chicago Mr. Moody saw a little girl standing on the street with a pail in her hand. He went up to her and invited her to his Sunday school, telling her what a pleasant place it was. She promised to go the following Sunday, but she did not do so. Mr. Moody watched for her for weeks, and then one day he saw her on the street again, at some distance from him. He started toward her, but she saw him too and started to run away. Mr. Moody followed her. She went down one street, with Mr. Moody after her; she went up another street, with Mr. Moody after her, through an alley, Mr. Moody still following; out on another street, Mr. Moody after her; then she dashed into a saloon and Mr. Moody dashed after her. She ran out the back door and up a flight of stairs, Mr. Moody still following; she dashed into a room, Mr. Moody following; she threw herself under the bed and Mr. Moody reached under the bed and pulled her out by the foot, and led her to Christ.

He found that her mother was a widow who had once seen better circumstances, but had gone down until now she was living over this saloon. She had several children. Mr. Moody led the mother and all the family to Christ. Several of the children were prominent members of the Moody Church until they moved away, and afterwards became prominent in churches elsewhere. This particular child, whom he pulled from underneath the bed, was, when I was the pastor of the Moody Church, the wife of one of the most prominent officers in the church.

Only two or three years ago, as I came out of a ticket office in Memphis, Tennessee, a fine-looking young man followed me. He said: "Are you not Dr. Torrey?" I said, "Yes." He said: "I am so and so." He was the son of this woman. He was then a travelling man, and an officer in the church where he lived. When Mr. Moody pulled that little child out from under the bed by the foot he was pulling a whole family into the Kingdom of God, and eternity alone will reveal how many succeeding generations he was pulling into the Kingdom of God.

D. L. Moody's consuming passion for souls was not for the souls of those who would be helpful to him in building up his work here or elsewhere; his love for souls knew no class limitations. He was no respecter of persons; it might be an earl or a duke or it might be an ignorant coloured boy on the street; it was all the same to him; there was a soul to save and he did what lay in his power to save that soul.

A friend once told me that the first time he ever heard of Mr. Moody was when Mr. Reynolds of Peoria told him that he once found Mr. Moody sitting in one of the squatters' shanties that used to be in that part of the city toward the lake, which was then called, "The Sands," with a coloured boy on his knee, a tallow candle in one hand and a Bible in the other, and Mr. Moody was spelling out the words (for at that time the boy could not read very well) of certain verses of Scripture, in an attempt to lead that ignorant coloured boy to Christ.

Oh, young men and women and all Christian workers, if you and I were on fire for souls like that, how long would it be before we had a revival? Suppose that tonight the fire of God falls and fills our hearts, a burning fire that will send us out all over the country, and across the water to China, Japan, India and Africa, to tell lost souls the way of salvation!

(7) DEFINITELY ENDUED WITH POWER FROM ON HIGH

The seventh thing that was the secret of why God used D. L. Moody was that he had a very definite enduement with power from on High, a very clear and definite baptism with the Holy Ghost. Moody knew he had "the baptism with the Holy Ghost"; he had no doubt about it. In his early days he was a great hustler; he had a tremendous desire to do something, but he had no real power. He worked very largely in the energy of the flesh.

But there were two humble Free Methodist women who used to come over to his meetings in the Y.M.C.A. One was "Auntie Cook" and the other, Mrs. Snow. (I think her name was not Snow at that time.) These two women would come to Mr. Moody at the close of his meetings and say: "We are praying for you." Finally, Mr. Moody became somewhat nettled and said to them one night: "Why are you praying for me? Why don't you pray for the unsaved?" They replied: "We are praying that you may get the power." Mr. Moody did not know what that meant, but he got to thinking about it, and then went to these women and said: "I wish you would tell me what you mean"; and they told him about the definite baptism with the Holy Ghost. Then he asked that he might pray with them and not they merely pray for him.

Auntie Cook once told me of the intense fervour with which Mr. Moody prayed on that occasion. She told me in words that I scarcely dare repeat, though I have never forgotten them. And he not only prayed with them, but he also prayed alone.

Not long after, one day on his way to England, he was walking up Wall Street in New York; (Mr. Moody very seldom told this and I almost hesitate to tell it) and in the midst of the bustle and hurry of that city his prayer was answered; the power of God fell upon him as he walked up the street and he had to hurry off to the house of a friend and ask that he might have a room by himself, and in that room he stayed alone for hours; and the Holy Ghost came upon him, filling his soul with such joy that at last he had to ask God to withhold His hand, lest he die on the spot from very joy. He went out from that place with the power of the Holy Ghost upon him, and when he got to London (partly through the prayers of a bedridden saint in Mr. Lessey's church), the power of God wrought through him mightily in North London, and hundreds were added to the churches; and that was what led to his being invited over to the wonderful campaign that followed in later years.

Time and again Mr. Moody would come to me and say: "Torrey, I want you to preach on the baptism with the Holy Ghost." I do not know how many times he asked me to speak on that subject. Once, when I had been invited to preach in the Fifth Avenue Presbyterian Church, New York (invited at Mr. Moody's suggestion; had it not been for his suggestion the invitation would never have been extended to me), just before I started for New York, Mr. Moody drove up to my house and said: "Torrey, they want you to preach at the Fifth Avenue Presbyterian Church in New York. It is a great big church, cost a million dollars to build it." Then he continued: "Torrey, I just want to ask one thing of you. I want to tell you what to preach about. You will preach that sermon of yours on 'Ten Reasons Why I Believe the Bible to Be the Word of God' and your sermon on 'The Baptism With the Holy Ghost.'"

Time and again, when a call came to me to go off to some church, he would come up to me and say: "Now, Torrey, be sure and preach on the baptism with the Holy Ghost." I do not know how many times he said that to me. Once I asked him: "Mr. Moody, don't you think I have any sermons but those two: 'Ten Reasons Why I Believe the Bible to Be the Word of God' and 'The Baptism With the Holy Ghost'?" "Never mind that," he replied, "you give them those two sermons."

Once he had some teachers at Northfield — fine men, all of them, but they did not believe in a definite baptism with the Holy Ghost for the individual. They believed that every child of God was baptized with the Holy Ghost, and they did not believe in any special baptism with the Holy Ghost for the individual. Mr. Moody came to me and said: "Torrey, will you come up to my house after the meeting tonight and I will get those men to come, and I want you to talk this thing out with them."

Of course, I very readily consented, and Mr. Moody and I talked for a long time, but they did not altogether see eye to eye with us. And when they went, Mr. Moody signalled me to remain for a few moments. Mr. Moody sat there with his chin on his breast, as he so often sat when he was in deep thought; then he looked up and said: "Oh, why will they split hairs? Why don't they see that this is just the one thing that they themselves need? They are good teachers, they are wonderful teachers, and I am so glad to have them here; but why will they not see that the baptism with the Holy Ghost is just the one touch that they themselves need?"

I shall never forget the eighth of July 1894, to my dying day. It was the closing day of the Northfield Students' Conference — the gathering of the students from the eastern colleges. Mr. Moody had asked me to preach on Saturday night and Sunday morning on the baptism with the Holy Ghost. On Saturday night I had spoken about, "The Baptism With the Holy Ghost: What It Is; What It Does; the Need of It and the Possibility of It." On Sunday morning I spoke on "The Baptism With the Holy Spirit: How to Get It." It was just exactly twelve o'clock when I finished my morning sermon, and I took out my watch and said: "Mr. Moody has invited us all to go up to the mountain at three o'clock this afternoon to pray for the power of the Holy Spirit. It is three hours to three o'clock. Some of you cannot wait three hours. You do not need to wait. Go to your rooms; go out into the woods; go to your tent; go anywhere where you can get alone with God and have this matter out with Him."

At three o'clock we all gathered in front of Mr. Moody's mother's house (she was then still living), and then began to pass down the lane, through the gate, up on the mountainside. There were four hundred and fifty-six of us in all; I know the number because Paul Moody counted us as we passed through the gate.

After a while Mr. Moody said: "I don't think we need to go any further; let us sit down here." We sat down on stumps and logs and on the ground. Mr. Moody said: "Have any of you students anything to say?" I think about seventy-five of them arose, one after the other, and said: "Mr. Moody, I could not wait till three o'clock; I have been alone with God since the morning service, and I believe I have a right to say that I have been baptized with the Holy Spirit."

When these testimonies were over, Mr. Moody said: "Young men, I can't see any reason why we shouldn't kneel down here right now and ask God that the Holy Ghost may fall upon us just as definitely as He fell upon the apostles on the Day of Pentecost. Let us pray." And we did pray, there on the mountainside. As we had gone up the mountainside heavy clouds had been gathering, and just as we began to pray those clouds broke and the raindrops began to fall through the overhanging pines. But there was another cloud that had been gathering over Northfield for ten days, a cloud big with the mercy and grace and power of God; and as we began to pray our prayers seemed to pierce that cloud and the Holy Ghost fell upon us. Men and women, that is what we all need the Baptism with the Holy Ghost.